The E◆Z Legal Guide to

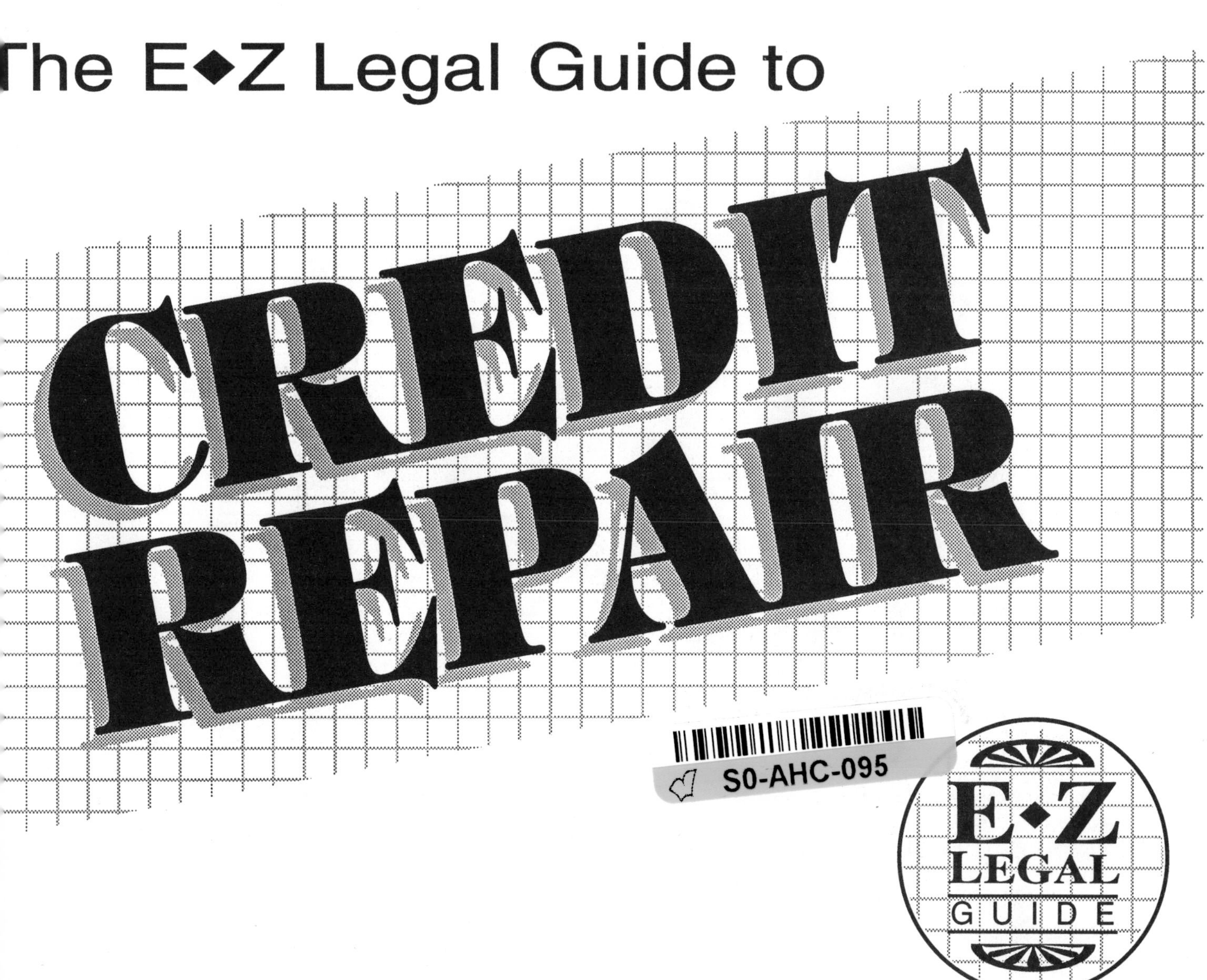

E◆Z Legal Forms
Deerfield Beach, Florida

... when you need it in writing!™

Distributed by E-Z Legal Forms, Inc.
Manufactured in the United States of America

1 2 3 4 5 6 7 8 9 10 **CPC**

This book is sold with the understanding that neither the author nor the publisher is engaged in rendering legal advice. If legal advice is required, the services of an attorney should be sought. Publisher and author cannot in any way guarantee that the forms in this book are being used for the purposes intended and, therefore, assume no responsibility for their proper and correct use.

Library of Congress Catalog Card Number: 94-061810

The E-Z Legal Guide to Credit Repair
p. cm.

ISBN 1-56382-403-5: $14.95

Title: The E-Z Legal Guide to Credit Repair.

Credit Repair

Important Facts

E-Z Legal products are designed to provide authoritative and accurate information in regard to the subject matter covered. However, neither this nor any other publication can take the place of an attorney on important legal matters.

Information in this guide has been carefully compiled from sources believed to be reliable, but the accuracy of the information is not guaranteed, as laws and regulations may change or be subject to differing interpretations.

Why not have your attorney review this guide? We encourage it.

Limited Warranty and Disclaimer

This is a self-help legal product and is intended to be used by the consumer for his or her own benefit. Use of this product to benefit a second party may be considered the unauthorized practice of law.

As with any legal matter, common sense should determine whether you need the assistance of an attorney. We urge you to consult with an attorney whenever large amounts of money are involved or on any matter when you do not understand how to properly complete a form or question its adequacy to protect you.

It is understood that by using this legal guide you are acting as your own attorney. Accordingly, the publisher, author, distributor and retailer shall have neither liability nor responsibility to any party for any loss or damage caused or alleged to be caused by use of this guide. This guide is sold with the understanding that the publisher, author, distributor and retailer are not engaged in rendering legal services. If legal services or other expert assistance are required, the services of a competent professional should be sought.

PRINTED IN THE
UNITED STATES
OF AMERICA

E•Z LEGAL FORMS®

384 South Military Trail
Deerfield Beach, FL 33442
Tel. 305-480-8933
Fax 305-480-8906

Money-back guarantee

E-Z Legal Forms offers you a limited guarantee. If you consider E-Z Legal Forms to be defective in any way, you may return your purchase to us within 30 days for a full refund of the list or purchase price, whichever is lower. In no event shall our liability – or the liability of any retailer – exceed the purchase price of the product. Use of the product constitutes acceptance of these terms.

Copyright Permission Certificate

The purchaser of this guide is hereby authorized to reproduce in any form or by any means, electronic or mechanical, including photocopying, all forms and documents contained in this guide, provided it is for nonprofit, educational or private use. Such reproduction requires no further permission from the publisher and/or payment of any permission fee.

The reproduction of any form or document in any other publication intended for sale is prohibited without the written permission of the publisher.

Publication for nonprofit use should provide proper attribution to E-Z Legal Forms.

Barry R. Chesler, President, E-Z Legal Forms

Credit Repair

Table of contents

How to use this E-Z Legal Guide 7

Introduction 9

1 Test your creditworthiness 11

2 How to develop triple-A credit 17

3 Obtaining credit 23

4 What you credit report discloses 35

5 The 10-step strategy to repairing your credit 39

6 Gain creditor cooperation 51

7 How to turn current financial problems into a positive credit rating 57

The forms in this guide 65

Fair Credit Reporting Act 79

Glossary of useful terms 95

How to Save on Attorney Fees 99

Index 123

How to use this E-Z Legal Guide

E-Z Legal Guides can help you achieve an important legal objective conveniently, efficiently and economically. But it is nevertheless important for you to properly use this guide if you are to avoid later difficulties.

Step-by-step instructions for using this guide:

1 Carefully read all information, warnings and disclaimers concerning the legal forms in this guide. If after thorough examination you decide that you have circumstances that are not covered by the forms in this guide, or you do not feel confident about preparing your own documents, consult an attorney.

2 Before filling out a form, make several copies of the original to practice on, and for future use and updates. You should also make copies of the completed forms. Create a record-keeping system for both sets of copies.

3 Complete each blank on each legal form. Do not skip over inapplicable blanks or lines intended to be completed. If the blank is inapplicable, mark "N/A" or "None" or use a dash. This shows you have not overlooked the item.

4 Always use pen or type on legal documents. Never use pencil.

5 Avoid erasing or crossing out anything you've written on final documents.

6 It is important to remember that on legal contracts or agreements between parties all terms and conditions must be clearly stated. Provisions may not be enforceable unless in writing. All parties to the agreement should receive a copy.

7 You may find more specific instructions within this guide for completing some forms. These instructions are for your benefit and protection, so follow them closely.

8 You will find a helpful glossary of terms at the end of this guide. Refer to this glossary if you encounter unfamiliar terms.

9 Always keep legal documents in a safe place and in a location known to your spouse, family, executor or attorney.

Good credit is essential in America today because so many of the things we want to buy must be financed or bought on credit. And once you have a bad credit rating, it is nearly impossible to avoid detection. A vast network of credit reporting agencies keeps track of every American who does business or buys on credit. These agencies are the gatekeepers of credit. Each time you apply for credit through a bank, store or credit card agency, the prospective lender typically checks your current credit rating with one or more of these agencies.

There are nearly 2,000 credit bureaus in the United States, but there are only a few large regional bureaus. The top ones are TRW, Trans Union, CSC, and CBI. TRW, the largest with approximately 80 million credit files in storage, has processed over 35 million credit reports in the last year and boasts 50,000 business subscribers.

"Subscribers" are the many businesses that pay to obtain the credit information contained in a bureau's files. Subscribers rightfully believe that the information contained in your credit file is a good indication of your creditworthiness. How you have paid other creditors in the past is an indication of how you may act in the future. Subscribers also use your credit file to verify information you have provided on your credit application.

Usually the same potential creditors who receive information about you also provide information to the credit bureaus. When you fill out an application for credit from a bank, store or credit card company, that information is forwarded to the bureau, along with constant updates on the status of your account. But not all creditors report what they know about you to the credit bureaus. And of those that do, not all report the entire contents of their files.

Creditors who deal with the credit bureaus most often, for purposes of both receiving and issuing information, are the commercial banks, including their credit card departments; credit card companies; larger savings and loans; major department stores and finance companies.

What accounts are usually not reported? Utilities, hospitals, mortgages, credit unions, oil company credit cards and checking and savings account information. This means, for example, there is little chance your bounced check history will be reported.

For businesses that report to these credit bureaus, transfer of account information is a simple matter of sending the bureau computer disks every month or quarter, transmitted either physically or over telephone lines. The disks contain the account information and any changes and additions to be made to your credit file, and thus ensure continuously updated credit profiles.

This guide will show you how to access your credit report, and how to make these frequent updates work to your advantage. Start today to build the credit rating you want!

CHAPTER

Test your creditworthiness

The secret to winning credit is building a good credit rating. A good credit history shows the ability and willingness to repay a loan.

Consider these four key points concerning credit:

1) A credit rating is based on your credit history, which is a record indicating your trustworthiness and ability to repay a loan.

2) Credit ratings are nothing more than an attempt to estimate your ability and willingness to repay a loan or debt.

3) Creditors report your loan activities to the credit bureaus. They are allowed to report your repayment history as delinquent (negative), regular (positive), or neutral (non-rated).

4) No credit bureau is allowed to evaluate your ability to repay a loan.

Creditors have the privilege to rate you privately, but are prevented from publishing their evaluations.

How to measure your credit rating

Your credit rating is a composite of the information contained in your credit report plus the information provided directly to the lender. Lenders use three types of information to determine your credit rating:

1) ***The lender's personal evaluation*** of your potential. Objective criteria give the lending institution a pretty good idea of how you stack up as a credit risk. Borrowers, however, often seek amounts beyond their credit limit. The lending institution leaves it up to the loan officer to pass judg-

ment concerning the fine points of a loan decision, based on his or her professional interpretation of the objective data provided by the credit report scoring system and the "20 percent rule."

2) ***Short-term-debt-to-income ratio*** using the 20 percent rule. Lenders will calculate what percentage of your annual income your short-term debt represents. (Long-term debt, like a mortgage, is excluded from consideration here.) You are generally allowed no more short-term debt than 15 to 20 percent of your total annual income.

3) ***A credit scoring system.*** Banks and similar large lending institutions, such as finance companies, savings and loan companies and credit unions, generally employ a scoring system used to rate your creditworthiness. An example of such a scoring system is provided in this chapter. By knowing how you will be evaluated, you can begin now to substantially improve your credit rating. You will discover weak points that stand in need of improvement as well as positive points that can be emphasized. In addition, you will know the amount of credit for which you qualify given your income, net worth, credit record and other relevant factors.

Highlight

You are generally allowed no more short-term debt than 15 to 20 percent of your total annual income.

Take two steps

There are two steps you should take before you attempt to improve your creditworthiness.

Step 1. Before applying for any credit, check your credit report to be sure that there are no negative marks on it. Even if you are new to the world of credit or strongly believe that your credit rating is very good already, check your report to be absolutely certain.

Negative marks tend to show up more consistently than positive marks because creditors hire credit bureaus to prevent them from making bad loans. Naturally, creditors and credit bureaus are more likely to seek out and report negative information.

You want to be sure that prospective lenders see only positive things being reported about you. So you must first repair the negative marks. Then begin to build a positive credit history.

In addition to having no negative marks, you must have a positive credit history that establishes your track record.

Step 2. Score yourself. Most lenders use a scoring system to establish the level of your credit ability. A loan officer or board will disqualify applicants who do not achieve a minimum number of points on the credit scoring test. The number of points required is predetermined by the lender's policymaking committee. Then it is given to the officer, who uses it as a guideline in determining whether a loan should be approved.

Lending institutions utilize standardized scoring systems to make the process of approving loans more objective. For instance, banks know from experience that individuals at a certain salary level can handle a combined credit line of a certain amount on their credit cards. Lenders have also found that people who move frequently, don't have telephones or can't keep steady jobs are poor credit risks. Questions on the scoring test clearly reveal your salary level and patterns of living.

Highlights

By knowing precisely what lenders are looking for, you can identify areas in your credit profile that need improvement, pinpoint strengths and adjust your credit image.

While the loan officer's personal judgment of the borrower is important, banks try not to rely too much on the banker's subjective evaluation of the borrower. By following the objective standards set by the scoring system, the banks make fewer bad loans.

Although each lender has its own system and asks its own questions, the key questions are universal. By knowing precisely what lenders are looking for, you can identify areas in your credit profile that need improvement, pinpoint strengths and adjust your credit image.

Test yourself with this scoring system

Factors	Points
1) Years at present job:	
a) Less than one year	0
b) One to two years	1
c) Two to four years	2
d) Four to ten years	3
e) Over ten years	4
2) Monthly income level:	
a) Less than $1,000	0
b) $1,000 to $1,500	1
c) $1,500 to $2,000	2
d) Over $2,000	3
3) Present obligations past due:	
a) Yes	0
b) No	1

Factors	Points
4) Total monthly debt payments compared to income (after taxes):	
a) 50%	0
b) 40% to 49%	1
c) 30% to 39%	2
d) under 30%	3
5) Prior loans with lender:	
a) No	0
b) Yes, but not closed	0
c) Yes, but closed with two or fewer 11-day notices per year	1
6) Checking account:	
a) None	0
b) Yes, but with over five rejected items over past year	1
c) Yes, but with no rejected items over past year	2
7) Length at present or previous address:	
a) Less than three years	0
b) Three years or more	1
8) Age of newest automobile:	
a) Over one year old	0
b) Less than one year old	1
9) Savings account with lender:	
a) No	0
b) Yes	1
10) Own real estate:	
a) No	0
b) Yes	3
11) Telephone in own name:	
a) No	0
b) Yes	1

Factors	Points
12) Good credit references:	
a) No	0
b) Yes	1

These questions, or something very close to them, appear on most credit scoring systems. The questions are selected and the points assigned by the bank's Consumer Credit Policy Committee. The policy committee then prepares a set of guidelines for applying the scoring system to guide the loan officer. Not only will this scoring system vary from bank to bank, but even within the same bank the criteria will change, depending on national and regional economic conditions and the bank's own competitive position. Obviously, when loan money is abundant, the criteria will not be as strict as when loan money is tight.

Highlights

If you fall in the lowest category, your application will be rejected outright. But don't give up hope.

Now put your score in perspective. The guidelines provided to the loan officer might read like this:

0-50 percent of possible points: Reject outright. Don't waste time on this application.

50-60 percent of possible points: Review very carefully. Do not approve unless there are other good reasons indicating that credit should be granted.

60-70 percent of possible points: Review with a bias toward approval. (This is the profile of the typical consumer and indicates a reasonable risk.)

70-90 percent of possible points: Grant the loan unless there is good reason to deny.

90-100 percent of possible points: Automatically grant credit within reasonable limits.

If you fall in the lowest category, your application will be rejected outright. But don't give up hope. You may be able to obtain a small loan with some collateral, or perhaps by finding a co-signer. (A co-signer uses his credit to guarantee yours by accepting responsibility to make good on the loan if you don't.) An example of this applicant might be a student without steady employment or a permanent address who may be able to obtain a car loan if his parents co-sign.

If you fall in the 50-90 percent categories, you can expect a full review of your application for credit. Someone in the lower range of this category may require a co-signer and/or collateral. If you are in the 90-100 percent range you can generally get unsecured credit on your signature alone.

Think about this scoring system. Obviously, each bank keeps its point system secret. Only a loan officer knows how many points you need to pass the minimum requirement for credit approval. But you can improve your chances for winning credit once you know the system.

Highlight

You can improve your chances for winning credit once you know the system.

CHAPTER

How to develop triple-A credit

There are many ways to improve your chances for obtaining credit. Here are five of the most important tips.

Tip 1. Know the 20 percent rule

Apply only for credit you can handle. Add up all your short-term debts, like installment loans and credit card balances, outstanding telephone bills if they are large, and notes due in a year or so. Exclude your long-term debts, like mortgages. Then figure your annual income from all sources. Divide your annual income into your total short-term debts.

If the answer is 0.20 or greater, then you are borrowed to the limit that is generally considered safe, referred to as the 20-percent rule. If you are below 0.20, then theoretically you can borrow an amount which, when added to your short-term debt and divided by your annual income, would yield 0.20, or 20 percent.

For example, if your annual income is $25,000 and your short-term debt is $5,000, you are at the 20 percent level and are pretty well borrowed to your limit. But if your short-term debt is only $2,000, then you may have about $3,000 that is still borrowable.

Tip 2. Accentuate the positive

Emphasize why credit should be granted. When filling out credit applications, emphasize those features of your credit record that indicate your credit strength. It is important to capitalize on your strong points by making them the focus of your credit strategy.

A good income history is one of the strongest points you can make. A good track record at the credit bureaus, with your banking institution and with creditors such as the telephone company and utilities goes a long way toward making you look good. Lenders like to see evidence of earning power over a period of time, as well as a consistent record of making payments on time.

Notice, when you are filling out your applications for credit, that requests for information are much the same from application to application. To organize yourself for completing credit applications, use the Master Credit Data form provided at the end of this chapter.

The Master Credit Data form fulfills another purpose. It allows you to submit uniform applications and provides a ready reference in case a creditor calls with further questions.

In addition, the Master Credit Data form helps you put your best foot forward by selecting the most appropriate data to provide to a lender's questions. While you must answer all questions truthfully and completely, there are often different ways the same question can be honestly answered. Choose the way that is most favorable to you.

Highlight

While you must answer all questions truthfully and completely, there are often different ways the same question can be honestly answered. Choose the way that is most favorable to you.

A word of caution: Never be dishonest when filling out an application for credit. To knowingly misrepresent yourself on a credit application is fraud, and a serious offense.

But being selective is not being dishonest. Lenders are very aware of how financial data can be arranged to appear better or worse. They expect you to put your best foot forward, within reason. If you don't, they may believe your financial situation is worse then it actually is. For example, if you fail to check out your credit references and someone you list provides a poor reference, the lender is likely to conclude that that was the best you could do.

Tip 3. Get a secured credit card

If you don't yet qualify for an ordinary or unsecured credit card, obtain a secured Visa or MasterCard. A secured credit card is the doorway to establishing a track record of creditworthiness.

A secured credit card has a credit limit based on your cash deposit. A minimum deposit must be kept in a savings account and you only have partial access to this money. In other words, your credit line will vary from 50 percent to 100 percent of the minimum deposit secured by your savings account balance, which you agree to leave untouched while you have the secured credit card.

An annual fee will probably be charged for the card. The annual percentage rate may be lower than the industry average, though, since it is backed by collateral. However, some institutions charge an additional processing fee of about $50. This fee may be refundable if the card is not granted.

Highlight

Borrowing from a bank need not be difficult. Bankers need customers just as much as customers need bankers, so don't let their formality intimidate you.

The best places to obtain secured credit cards are through the highly competitive big national banks, your own local bank where you have cultivated the trust of the loan officer, or savings and loan institutions in your state. The S&Ls will vary widely in their policies, but are worth a try.

Tip 4. Get a retailer's credit card

Apply for credit from local and national retailers. You need only a few of these cards to establish a good credit record.

In many cases, your secured Visa or MasterCard will get you almost instant approval for a department store credit card, or charge account. Secured cards look exactly the same as ordinary cards so no one is likely to suspect that your card is secured unless you tell them. It is often easiest to win credit from retailers. Use their references to secure additional credit from others once you have established your creditworthiness.

Tip 5. Open a checking account

Once you have chosen a bank you would like to work with, establish credit with a checking account. Make your initial deposit as large as possible. During the next few months, when potential lenders check your credit with your bank, they will learn only of your initial deposit. After a few months of deposits and withdrawals, your average daily balance for the month will be reported to creditors who request credit information. If you don't have the cash on hand to open this account yourself, borrow from relatives or friends. Make this a short-term loan and pay it back in the form of a check once the account is established. Start off on the right step: Keep this new account balanced and never overdraw your account.

How to successfully borrow from a bank

Borrowing from a bank need not be difficult. Bankers need customers just as much as customers need bankers, so don't let their formality intimidate you. Bankers like to be in control of the situation, because they are responsible for handling money that is not their own. They give the impression that banking is serious business because it is a serious business. Lending another person's money, on their part, and borrowing money, on yours, involves a lot of responsibility on both sides.

However, don't let the formality and responsibility get in your way, or prevent you from dealing effectively. Bankers are people just like you.

Bankers are also businesspeople. If they see that you are well-groomed and appear reasonably intelligent and responsible, they will take you more seriously. If you appear to be a choice customer, they will jump at the chance to serve you.

Highlight

As you grow in ability as a credit entrepreneur, you will need a good relationship with a local banker, so start developing it now.

Remember, banks make their money by making loans. As a responsible person, you are quite important to them.

As you grow in ability as a credit entrepreneur, you will need a good relationship with a local banker, so start developing it now. But a good banking relationship can help you do more than obtain a loan.

In addition, bankers are very knowledgeable about the credit world. Their job is to extend credit to creditworthy people. By asking him or her the right questions, you can use your local banker as a free consulting service. Your banker will be happy to give you the advice you need in order to get your business.

Keep these points in mind

1) Your own bank may be best. If you have a good banking relationship with your local bank, start there. A local bank offers you the opportunity to develop a good credit history. If you have a good relationship with your own banker, you have a slight edge over the prospective borrower who has no personal connection with his bank. Bankers can bend rules if they feel confident about you, even if there are several questionable marks on your credit record, or your income isn't quite high enough to justify the loan you want.

2) Even if it's not your current bank, choose a local bank. You will, in time, be applying to nationwide banks for many of your loans or credit cards. Citibank and Bank of America may not be in your neighborhood, nor do you need to start your quest for credit through them. For now, a local bank is adequate to start the ball rolling. Furthermore, local bankers are likely to be more receptive and pay more attention to you.

3) Investigate many banks. Even though you are focusing on a particular local bank, you should contact many banks in your area. If you are developing ties with a dozen banks simultaneously, the odds are good that one bank will come through with the credit you need. Nationwide banks may be too distant to visit in person. You can, however, contact them by mail. Many also have toll-free telephone numbers to enable you to get in touch personally. If yours doesn't have an 800 number and you do any significant business with it, the loan officer will be happy to accept collect calls.

Highlight

Never think of yourself as going to a bank to ask a favor. You are a knowledgeable customer coming to discuss advantageous terms.

4) Establish a personal relationship with a loan officer. Bankers pick up on positive personality traits and, quite often, favor you with the benefit of the doubt. To gain the banker's personal respect, you must establish a personal rapport with him. It's important to deal with the individual loan officer with whom you feel most comfortable.

5) Don't be intimidated. Never think of yourself as going to a bank to ask a favor. You are a knowledgeable customer coming to discuss advantageous terms.

Your meetings with bankers will further educate you in the ways of the banking world. Just as an expert chess player becomes a master through playing many different opponents again and again, the more contact you have with banks and other lenders the more you will learn. As you develop your credit relationships, you will locate more banks and lenders anxious to extend credit to you.

MASTER CREDIT DATA

Name____

Address____

____

Phone____________________

Previous Address __________________________________

____

How Long There? __________

Other Names Credit Obtained Under ___________

____

Date of Birth______________________________________

Social Security Number_____________________________

Driver's License Number and State__________________

Employer's Name__________________________________

Employer's Address________________________________

____

How Long With This Employer? ____________________

Position Held ____________________

Supervisor______________________

Previous Employer's Name__________________________

Previous Employer's Address________________________

____

How Long With This Employer? ____________________

Position Held ____________________

Supervisor______________________

Number of Dependents______________

Weekly/Monthly Income From Job___________________

Other Income (state sources)_______________________

____

Closest Relative Not Living With You_______________

Address ____

____

Phone______________ Relationship________________

Alimony, Child Support or Maintenance Payments (only if being reported as source of income) ___________

Bank Accounts at this Bank__________________________

Other Bank Accounts_______________________________

____

Real Estate Owned/Rented___________________________

Name of Landlord or Mortgage Holder_______________

Address____

____

Phone________________________

Name of Titleholder________________________________

Current Value__________Mortgage Balance__________

Monthly Payment/Rent _____________________________

Year, Make and Model of Automobile(s)_____________

Where Financed____________________________________

Amount Owed__________Payments_______________

Have You Ever Filed Bankruptcy or Chapter 13? ________

When?________________________

Unsatisfied Judgments_______________________________

Are You a Co-Signer, Endorser or Guarantor for Others? __

____

Outstanding Lawsuits__________________________

CREDIT HISTORY

Creditor ____

Creditor's Address__________________________________

____

Name Account is Under_______________________________

Date Opened______________Credit Status__________

Unpaid Balance___________Monthly Payment________

Creditor ____

Creditor's Address__________________________________

____

Name Account is Under_______________________________

Date Opened______________Credit Status __________

Unpaid Balance___________Monthly Payment________

Creditor ____

Creditor's Address__________________________________

____

Name Account is Under_______________________________

Date Opened______________Credit Status __________

Unpaid Balance___________ Monthly Payment________

Creditor ____

Creditor's Address__________________________________

____

Name Account is Under_______________________________

Date Opened______________Credit Status __________

Unpaid Balance___________Monthly Payment________

Creditor ____

Creditor's Address__________________________________

Name Account is Under_______________________________

Date Opened______________ Credit Status __________

Unpaid Balance___________ Monthly Payment________

Creditor ____

Creditor's Address__________________________________

____

Name Account is Under_______________________________

Date Opened______________Credit Status __________

Unpaid Balance___________Monthly Payment________

CHAPTER

Obtaining credit

Most people emerging from financial difficulties consider it top priority to obtain credit cards, such as Visa and MasterCard, through which they can again charge day-to-day purchases.

Although it is possible to get a credit card without a good credit history or a high income, few people know how to do it. Most go through the ordinary channels and get turned down. Therefore, they incorrectly conclude that a Visa or MasterCard is unavailable to them.

Sometimes people with good credit histories and high incomes get turned down when they apply for several cards, yet they hear of people who seem less creditworthy who carry numerous cards.

The credit card world can be pretty simple when you understand the rules it works by, but it is quite challenging, and even mysterious, to the uninformed.

How the credit card system works

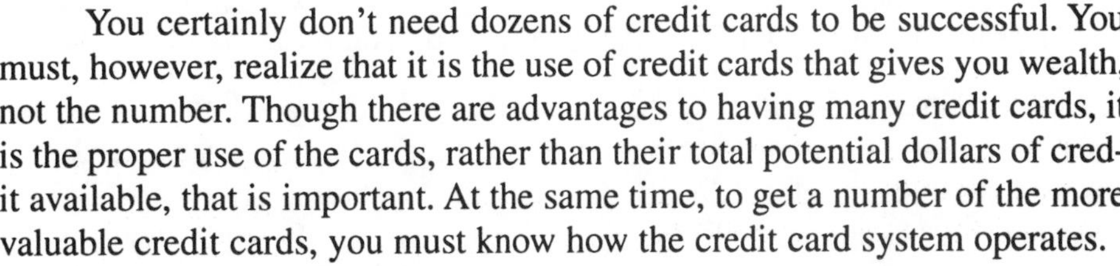

You certainly don't need dozens of credit cards to be successful. You must, however, realize that it is the use of credit cards that gives you wealth, not the number. Though there are advantages to having many credit cards, it is the proper use of the cards, rather than their total potential dollars of credit available, that is important. At the same time, to get a number of the more valuable credit cards, you must know how the credit card system operates.

By studying the way the banks interrelate, you will understand how to deal with credit card companies. You will find that banks work together to keep track of their cardholders. Most banks want to know how many credit cards you have before considering you for one of their own cards.

Nor will every lending institution issue you a credit card. This is because many banks share a computer connection that trades vital cardholder information. When banks become aware that you have "too many" cards (each bank has its own policy on how many cards is too many), they automatically reject your applications.

Furthermore, many banks offer the same card, and usually disallow repeat cards to be issued to a cardholder. You may, therefore, receive only one card from this interconnected network of cooperating banks.

Highlight

When banks become aware that you have "too many" cards (each bank has its own policy on how many cards is too many), they automatically reject your applications.

To make this clear, let's examine what might hypothetically be called the Bank Card System. When you apply for a credit card at your local bank, much more is going on than you realize. Although the name of your local bank may be proudly displayed on your card, chances are your card was issued by another bank working behind the scenes.

Because banks are interconnected, they trade favors and reciprocate functions. Most often, however, banks hire each other to perform different services and, as a result, create economies and save themselves money.

Processing an application for a bank credit card requires a bank to perform many functions it normally cannot afford to do on its own. So it seeks outside assistance by using other banks.

This Bank Card System is complicated. Cardholders rarely gain insight into how involved the card-issuing process can be. First there is the process of accepting the new applications, asking for credit reports, and setting up the approved accounts. Then there is card printing and embossing, as well as ongoing paperwork encompassing year after year of statements, sales brochures, late payment notices, and countless other details that make a credit card program successful.

Most banks cannot afford to support all the functions required to issue and follow through on credit cards. Therefore, to avoid the complicated and costly process, smaller banks act as credit card agents for the larger banks.

In other words, smaller banks contract with larger banks for card-related services. Many service packages are available. The largest card-processing centers therefore do all the accounting, credit checks, mailings, statements, collections, and administrative details for the small banks. The fee that the smaller bank pays is a percentage of the annual credit volume.

Most banks enjoy and benefit from this relationship. However, many more banks are now purchasing their own computer systems to cash in on the big profits that come from functioning as a large credit card processing center.

The main advantage of the Bank Card System is that it allows the smaller banks to stay in the game. This saves the small bank from having to invest in computers and more personnel to compete. Because of fierce interbank competition, most banks must offer their customers the convenience of credit cards. This is such an important part of bank promotion that many banks make their credit card package a major advertising tool to attract new customers from the competition.

Highlight

What happens if you simultaneously apply for credit cards to a dozen banks in your area? Inevitably, although through different chains, many of the banks will be connected to the same major bank.

The larger banks also benefit from the Bank Card System, because their overhead is partially subsidized by collecting the annual service fees from the smaller institutions using their card-processing services. In fact, card processing centers often realize handsome profits.

Some bank networks link different parts of the credit card process in a kind of chain. One bank may offer the card while another does the credit checks and a third (or fourth) does the card embossing and monthly statements. Some of these chains may be short and some may be surprisingly long. Interestingly, most major banks may have many lines of agent banks stretching out in chains under them. Some of these chains extend through as many as three or four successive agent banks.

Now, what happens if you simultaneously apply for credit cards to a dozen banks in your area? Inevitably, although through different chains, many of the banks will be connected to the same major bank. This raises two possibilities:

1) **The major bank may have a relationship** with the agent banks that prevents an applicant from obtaining more than one card from the major bank. In other words, if you apply to 12 banks that are connected to the same major bank, the major bank will only issue you one account. Therefore, only one credit card will result from your efforts.

Duplicate accounts are seldom allowed. Of the 12 applications processed by the major bank, the first one accepted becomes your account; 11 are automatically canceled out as they enter the main computerized system. The credit card will reflect the name of the bank that was on the accepted application. Unfortunately, however, you have needlessly generated 11 useless and potentially harmful inquiries on your credit report.

2) **The major bank may issue many cards** to the same individual if the agent banks assume responsibility for approving your credit, instead of

leaving it to the major bank. Furthermore, the agent banks would also have to assume responsibility for any defaults in payment.

Determining which chains do or do not issue duplicate cards requires some detective work, but is well worth the effort if your objective is to get more than one or two bank credit cards. Research in your geographic area of the country will give you greater insight into which Bank Card System can best serve your needs.

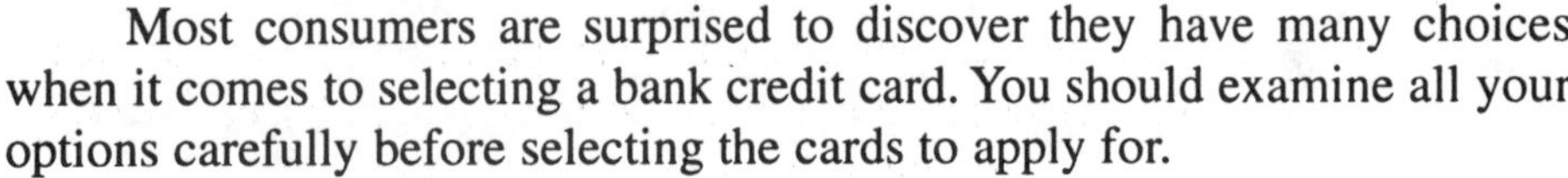

Shopping for credit cards

Highlight

There are great credit card bargains all over the nation – as well as deals you should avoid.

Most consumers are surprised to discover they have many choices when it comes to selecting a bank credit card. You should examine all your options carefully before selecting the cards to apply for.

Don't believe that all credit cards are alike. And don't be misled into believing that you must live in the same state to get a certain bank's credit card. Or that you must have an account with the bank.

You will learn that there are great credit card bargains all over the nation – as well as deals you should avoid. Compare bank policies before selecting your cards. The following three features are part of all bank card terms and should be reviewed before selecting a credit card:

1) **Transaction Fees.** Banks have discovered that 50 percent of all cardholders pay their total balance at the end of each month. This, naturally, limits the dollar amount of service fees each customer will be required to pay. To remedy this problem and increase revenue, some banks have designed transaction fees.

For example, a major California bank charges 12 cents for each use of the card. The cardholders felt they were getting a deal because the annual fee for this card was only $10 per year. However, for people who use their cards regularly, transaction fees can add up fast. It is important to check for transaction fees before applying for a bank card. Many cards charge no transaction fees, and may be far less costly than cards that impose fees.

2) **Annual Membership Fees.** Annual fees are designed to boost sagging credit card income for the banking industry. Because most people pay off their monthly statements before finance charges begin, banks feel that annual fees are vital for survival. However, some banks waive annual fees if you keep a minimum balance in your checking account. To evaluate the worth of this offer, check what the interest rate would be for your deposit. If it is too low, you would be losing income that could be made from a

deposit in another bank at a higher interest rate. The amount lost in interest may be greater than the money saved by not paying an annual membership fee.

3) **Finance Charges/Annual Percentage Rate (APR).** Rates vary between 11.5 percent and 22 percent, although each state has its legal ceiling. For instance, the District of Columbia limits interest rates to a maximum of 18 percent (and also disallows annual fees). Many credit card companies are now offering adjustable percentage rates based on the London Interbank Offered Rate (LIBOR) as a way to entice new cardholders to transfer existing card balances. Some of these rates are as low as 6.9 percent.

Highlight

Since a card in the hand is worth two in the bush, the new cardholder seldom has the willpower to return a new card, even one that arrives with a surprisingly high interest rate.

Many banks neglect to put their annual percentage rate on their application form. This is because their rates often change, based on other interest rate indicators and the interest charged by competition.

You often don't find out the actual interest rate you are asked to pay until the credit card arrives in the mail and you sign on the dotted line. Since a card in the hand is worth two in the bush, the new cardholder seldom has the willpower to return a new card, even one that arrives with a surprisingly high interest rate.

Two credit card features worth remembering

The credit card field is rapidly changing. Two recent features you should know about include:

1) **ATM Cards**. Plastic cards are issued by banks for use in Automatic Teller Machines (ATMs). You receive a personal identification number (PIN) with each card. Each card has a magnetic strip that is activated when you punch in your PIN.

Originally designed as cash dispensing cards, they now perform functions as diverse as deposits and withdrawals, cash advances on charge cards, bank transfers, account inquiries, and, surprisingly, bill payments.

Although a convenient method of banking, ATM plastic does not offer the same degree of consumer protection enjoyed by regular credit cards. For example, if you report a stolen ATM card within two days of the theft, you may face a maximum liability of $50. However, if the theft goes unreported, you may be held responsible for up to $500 of any resultant loss.

Also, unauthorized withdrawals must be reported within 60 days of their initial appearance on the bank statement or your liability is unlimited. In a situation like this, you could even lose your entire deposit.

The rule to follow when handling an ATM account is always to keep your PIN and ATM card separate.

2) **Debit Cards**. The debit card is a brother to the ATM card. Both cards are merely electronic replacements for a check. They do not represent an extension of credit.

Highlight

The debit card is a brother to the ATM card. Both cards are merely electronic replacements for a check. They do not represent an extension of credit.

Whereas the ATM card electronically draws cash in the same way a check can, the debit card replaces a check by paying bills and making purchases via an electronic hook-up with your account.

Bankers prefer debit cards over checks because check processing is generally unprofitable. If debit cards replace credit cards for purchases, however, bankers will lose finance charges normally collected on credit cards.

Merchants like the debit card system because they get their money immediately, electronically transferred into their company account. This system exists electronically, supported by a minimum of paperwork. Ideally, the merchant doesn't have to worry about a check being misplaced or lost, for example, or about a holdup in the store.

The process is not yet completely electronic. Debit card users still have to fill out paperwork similar to a sales slip or Master Card transcript when making a purchase. These slips are forwarded to the cardholder's bank or a third-party processor who has agreed to handle debit accounts, and then deducted from the cardholder's account in pretty much the same way a check is handled.

There is no debit system operating on a national scale. Merchants and banks have yet to agree on a standardized system. Experiments, however, have been initiated in Iowa, Florida and California to see if an electronic debit system is a viable addition to modern banking.

Because the debit card concept is so new, laws to define the cardholder's liability in the event of unauthorized use or theft are still evolving. Consult with the institution issuing the debit card to establish the terms of your liability.

13 essential tips for getting credit cards

1) **Assemble a list of banks from whom you will request applica-**

tion forms. Sometimes it's easier to get credit cards in the state you live in; the very large national banks are generally aggressive in seeking new accounts. Don't overlook savings and loan companies as well as credit unions in which you qualify for membership.

2) **Request an application form for Visa and MasterCard accounts, either by telephone or in writing**. Be certain to request information pertaining to finance charges and fees, because these are points often not included in the application. You will need this information to evaluate the institution's credit card policies.

Highlight

Do everything possible to remove the negative marks before you submit your application for credit.

3) **Obtain your credit report from the credit bureaus used by the credit card issuer to whom you are applying**. If your credit report reveals that you have some negative marks against you, follow the procedures outlined later in this guide to remove them.

Applying for credit with negative marks on your report invites refusal. Do everything possible to remove the negative marks before you submit your application for credit, following the procedures outlined in this guide. If your credit report lacks any details of your positive credit history, try to persuade the creditors to report that information to the credit bureau. The credit bureau can charge a fee for entering these reports, but it may be worth the expense if it allows you to improve your position in the credit world.

4) **Apply for a secured credit card if negative marks remain that can't be removed**. If you have gone through the credit repair procedures several times and negative marks such as bankruptcy, judgments, and delinquent payments remain, and you do not presently have any major credit cards, then apply for a secured card, following the instructions outlined in Chapter 2. Responsible use of a secured card will contribute to the building of a positive credit history. Meanwhile you can be repairing the dings in your credit rating, which then qualifies you for unsecured credit.

You may discover, however, that not all credit bureaus have negative reports on you. If you find a credit bureau that does not, apply for credit with an institution that uses this credit bureau and not with the ones with negative histories on you. Most of the large credit card issuers subscribe to the major credit reporting agencies, but you may be able to find a smaller institution that subscribes to the credit bureau you want.

5) **Apply for a secured card if your income is less than $1,000 a month**. If your total income from all sources is less than $1,000 a month, it may be difficult for you to get an unsecured credit card unless you score very high on all the other credit criteria and show that you can pay your debts from adequate assets.

However, to obtain even secured credit cards, you will generally need to show some income. The income does not need to be from a job. Pension or other retirement benefits, income from investments, or alimony may be sufficient.

The amount of credit you can qualify for is usually directly dependent on the amount of your income. If you want to enter the credit world on your terms, work at building your income. If you have no income, it is sometimes possible to get a credit card by obtaining a co-signer, someone who has good credit and agrees to assume responsibility for your debts.

Highlight

If you have no income, it is sometimes possible to get a credit card by obtaining a co-signer, someone who has good credit and agrees to assume responsibility for your debts.

6) **Get the number of inquiries on your credit report down to three or four in the past six months**. If you have a number of "active" inquiries – that is, inquiries that have been added to your report within the last six months – either wait until they automatically come off your report or attempt to remove them following the procedures outlined later in this guide.

7) **Apply for credit cards from retailers in your area**. Department store cards, gas company cards and other retail credit cards are usually fairly easy to obtain. Check to see whether your payments are reported to a credit bureau. Sometimes they are not, but if so, then using this card and repaying on time will boost your credit record.

Even if the payments on these accounts are not reported to a credit bureau, many applications for credit ask about your other credit card accounts. A good payment record on these more easily obtained accounts can give you some recommendations on which to build more credit. Often, having a secured Visa or MasterCard is sufficient to get credit from these other companies. They don't have elaborate credit-checking systems, so they will follow the lead of larger institutions that have already approved you.

8) **Have your loan officer assist you in getting a Visa or MasterCard. Ask what your chances are of qualifying at his or her institution**. Also ask what your chances are elsewhere. Different institutions have different policies and your loan officer is likely to know about them.

You may be advised to apply at another institution because it is more lenient in its credit requirements. Sometimes a lending institution will offer cards at a lower-than-average annual percentage rate, but tighten its requirements to reduce the chance of loss through bad loans. If this is the case with your bank, the loan officer may recommend that you go to another institution that charges higher rates but has more lenient credit requirements.

9) **Review the terms of the various card issuers, and decide what terms are important to you.** For example, if you are planning to use your credit cards to finance consumer purchases or investment opportunities, a low annual percentage rate is desirable. If, on the other hand, you are going to use a card for the convenience of day-to-day purchasing and intend to pay the full amount at the first billing to avoid finance charges, then a no annual fee card with a long grace period is what you are looking for.

The ideal, of course, is to get cards with no annual fee, low APR with a long grace period, and no other surcharges. You should realize, however, that banks are in business to make money, so no credit card provides all these advantages.

Highlight

The ideal is to get cards with no annual fee, low APR and a long grace period, with no other surcharges. However, banks are in business to make money, so no credit card provides all these advantages.

10) **Accurately complete your application forms for those credit cards that meet your requirements.** Answer all questions truthfully and completely, remembering that you are not required to give any more information than is requested. Type or print clearly. Use a street address – not a post office box number, care of, or general delivery. If you have a good credit record with a particular credit bureau, it is wise to attach a copy of that credit report to your application form.

11) **Don't send more than two or three applications at the same time to card issuers that use the same credit bureau.** This avoids being turned down for too many inquiries. Most credit card issuers will automatically request your credit report from the credit bureau when they receive your application. This will appear on future credit reports as inquiries. More than a few inquiries showing up in a short period may result in your being refused credit.

12) **Send out applications for unsecured credit cards to the card issuers you have targeted.** Record your responses and keep track of approvals, declines and requests for further information, as well as your response if called for.

13) **Request the reason for any credit declines and ask for the name of the credit bureau used.** If you are denied credit, federal law requires that you be told the reason in writing, as well as the identity of the credit bureau that was used.

You further have the right to request a free report from that credit bureau concerning the information contained in your file. You must respond to the rejection notice within 30 days to obtain this free credit report. (Order it only if you need one from that credit bureau, because your own requests generate inquiries, too, although these are usually not held against you.)

Determine exactly why you were refused credit. You have a right to know why you were turned down. Once you find out, you'll know exactly what you need to do to get approval, or at least to get to the next step of approval. If you don't understand the reason you were denied credit, contact the lending institution and ask for a specific reason so you can act on it using the strategies contained in this guide.

If you didn't pass the tests for unsecured credit, don't give up hope. Even if you have some negative marks on your credit report that you can't remove, it is still possible to get credit. It is also possible to get a loan with a low income level if there isn't a negative credit history. However, the loan must usually be secured with collateral.

Highlight

You have a right to know why you were turned down. Once you find out, you'll know exactly what you need to do to get approval, or at least to get to the next step of approval.

Remember, lenders want to lend money because they make money on the money they lend. But also remember that they make money only if the loan is repaid. Therefore, bank policy is strict and loan officers shy away from approving questionable loans. If your income is low or your credit history is either insufficient for evaluation or decidedly poor, you will not be approved for an unsecured credit card.

You may still qualify for a secured card. You may be a borderline case that doesn't qualify for unsecured credit but will qualify if some form of security or collateral is left with the lender to ensure payment. This is usually in the form of a savings account at the bank issuing the card (see Chapter 2).

There may be other forms of collateral acceptable to a bank: a pledge of stocks or bonds, a lien on an automobile or boat, or you may have other equally valuable collateral to use.

If you are unable to get a secured credit card on the strength of your collateral, try obtaining a card by having someone co-sign for you. The co-signer should have strong enough credit to act as security for the credit line on the card and some extra, just in case you turn out to be a poor risk. Becoming a co-signer is a big responsibility. Don't ask a person to co-sign for you if you can't live up to the obligations he or she will then be responsible for.

If you have some capital but a poor credit rating, you may consider a debit card as another type of secured credit card.

Debit cards look like ordinary Visa or MasterCards. When you use them, you do not receive credit, but your account gets charged. A debit card provides you the convenience of a credit card while allowing your funds to earn high interest in a money market account, for example. Many people use debit accounts like checking accounts. The big differences are, it is often easier to use a debit card than to write a check, and some places will accept debit cards but not checks.

A large brokerage firm can set you up with a debit card if you can open a money market account with it.

Your positive credit history using a secured credit card or a debit card may not be reported to the credit bureau. Your possession and responsible use of these cards does, however, create references that you can use in the future.

Highlight

Be a discriminating shopper. Find out what the best deals are before you select a credit card.

Compare credit card terms

Be a discriminating shopper. Find out what the best deals are before you select a credit card.

After you receive your application forms in the mail, go through each, looking for the following information:

1) What is the annual percentage rate used to compute finance charges?
2) Is there an annual fee? If so, how much?
3) What is the policy governing cash advances?
4) Are there any restrictions on how you may choose the card?
5) Is there a grace period before finance charges begin?
6) Does the bank compute finance charges by the adjusted balance method, the previous balance method, or the average daily balance method?
7) Does the bank originate its own cards or does another institution originate the cards?
8) Does the bank offer special services such as "prestige cards" or automatic teller machine (ATM) facilities?
9) What are the bank's collection practices and how lenient is it with borrower problems?

Credit card brokers

You may have noticed ads in national magazines guaranteeing Visa, MasterCard, or other credit cards even if you have a poor credit history. These companies are, in most cases, merely taking advantage of knowledge that the consumer may not yet have. They are simply furnishing applications for secured credit cards, sometimes collecting a non-refundable processing fee for doing so. Others send a booklet or an instructional sheet explaining secured credit cards. Save the $25 to $50 these firms charge. With the information in this chapter you are well prepared to obtain credit cards on your own.

Highlight

With the information in this chapter you are well prepared to obtain credit cards on your own.

CHAPTER

What your credit report discloses

Credit reports may vary slightly between agencies; however, most credit reports include:

1) **Identification information**: Your full name, last two addresses, Social Security number, date of birth, and place of employment if the credit bureau has received that information. Length of employment and income are typically not reported, but watch the former if it is reported, because it often is incorrect. Creditors will sometimes reject an application because they can't confirm employment. If you are self-employed, credit bureaus may have you listed as unemployed, which should be corrected immediately.

2) **Detailed information on the accounts listed**: Name of the issuer, date account was opened, original balance or limit, current balance (beginning with the reporting date, which is also listed), terms of account, and the current status of the account. The status of each item is indicated by a complicated code system that signifies exactly what has happened to the account. This leaves little room for guessing. It also leaves little room for paying a delinquent account and therefore changing your status so you are cleared. An example is CO NOW PAY, which means that the account was a charge off (CO) but you are now paying (NOW PAY).

3) **Public record information**: Bankruptcies, tax liens, judgments and other filings.

4) **Credit report requests**: Each time a creditor requests a copy of your report, it is recorded in your report and it stays on your record for up to one year. This addition is "non-evaluated" by the bureau, but it can be seen as negative if you have many inquiries with no subsequent accounts opened. Creditors who see this will assume you were turned down, even though there are other explanations for the inquiries.

5) **Consumer statement**: Finally, there is space on the report for you to place a consumer statement. This allows you to challenge or explain any creditor entry in your file in your own words.

5 common reasons for credit denial

When prospective lenders inquire about your credit standing, they examine your record with certain expectations. To evaluate your own report, you need to know those expectations. The five most common reasons for credit denial based on a credit report are as follows:

1) **Delinquent credit obligations**: Late payments, bad debts, or legal judgments against you make you look like a risky customer.

2) **Credit application incomplete**: Perhaps you left out some important information or made an error on the application. Any large discrepancy between your application and your credit file can count against you. The lender will wonder if you are hiding something.

3) **Too many inquiries**: Inquiries are made whenever you apply for credit. Seeing your own report also counts as an inquiry, but is usually not held against you. At the creditor's discretion, as few as four inquiries within six months' time may be considered a sign of excessive credit activity. The creditor may then presume that you are trying desperately to get credit and are being rejected elsewhere.

4) **Errors in your file**: These may arise simply from typing mistakes, or from confusing your name with someone else's similar name. If you have changed your address, this can also create problems in the recording of your credit history. Since the credit bureaus handle millions of files, the possibility for error is substantial. Errors can be found and corrected only by carefully reviewing your file for accuracy and then taking the necessary steps to correct any errors that you do find.

5) **Insufficient credit file**: Your credit history is too scanty for the type or amount of credit you requested. You need to develop your credit history more fully before qualifying for the level of credit you are now requesting.

Always examine your credit record before applying for credit. Periodic checking is important because credit bureaus can and do make mistakes in their credit information. They may confuse you with another individual, carry erroneous information in your file, or perhaps include false, incomplete or one-sided information provided by a creditor. Most of these problems can be resolved once you understand the procedures.

Highlight

Since the credit bureaus handle millions of files, the possibility for error is substantial.

Get a copy of your credit report 

It is easy to get copies of your records from those credit bureaus that have a report on you. The addresses of local offices can be found in the Yellow Pages of your phone book under Credit or Credit Rating and Reporting.

The following are the major nationwide credit reporting bureaus that may have a credit file on you:

Highlight

Write or call all four of the major credit reporting agencies, requesting a copy of your credit report.

1) **TRW Credit Information Service**
   Attn.: NCAC
   P.O. Box 2104
   Allen, TX 75002
   (214) 390-9191
   (800) 392-1122
2) **CSC Credit Services Inc.**
   652 E North Belt, Suite 400
   Houston TX 77060
   (713) 878-1900
3) **CBI/EQUIFAX**
   PO Box 105873
   Atlanta GA 30348
   (800) 685-1111
4) **Trans Union Corp.**
   PO Box 390
   Springville, PA 19064-0390
   (312) 408-1400
   (216) 779-7200

Write or call all four of the major credit reporting agencies, requesting a copy of your credit report. (See Sample 1) Forms corresponding to each sample are found in the back of this guide. In your letter, include your Social Security number. With the letter enclose a check for the proper amount (call to verify the exact amount required). Credit bureaus typically charge $10-$20 to issue a credit report.

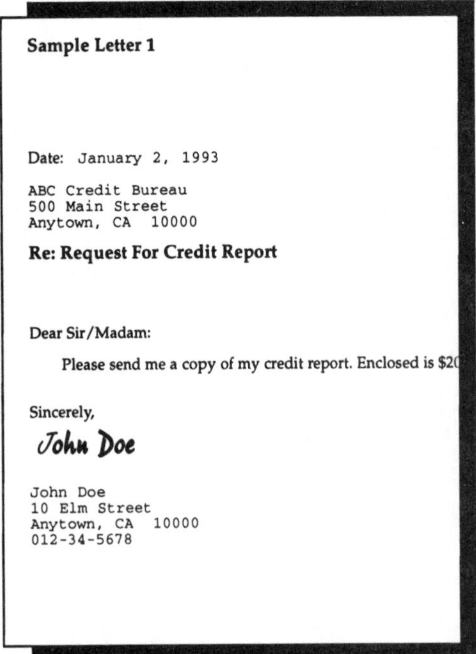

Sample Letter 1

Date: January 2, 1993

ABC Credit Bureau
500 Main Street
Anytown, CA 10000

Re: Request For Credit Report

Dear Sir/Madam:

Please send me a copy of my credit report. Enclosed is $2

Sincerely,

John Doe

John Doe
10 Elm Street
Anytown, CA 10000
012-34-5678

There are circumstances when you are entitled to a free copy of your credit report. For example, if you have received a credit rejection within the past 30 days, you may enclose a copy of the rejection to the credit bureau listed on the rejection letter and demand the bureau provide a free copy of your credit report. TRW now provides one free report annually to individuals regardless of their credit standing. Request a free credit report using Sample Letter 2.

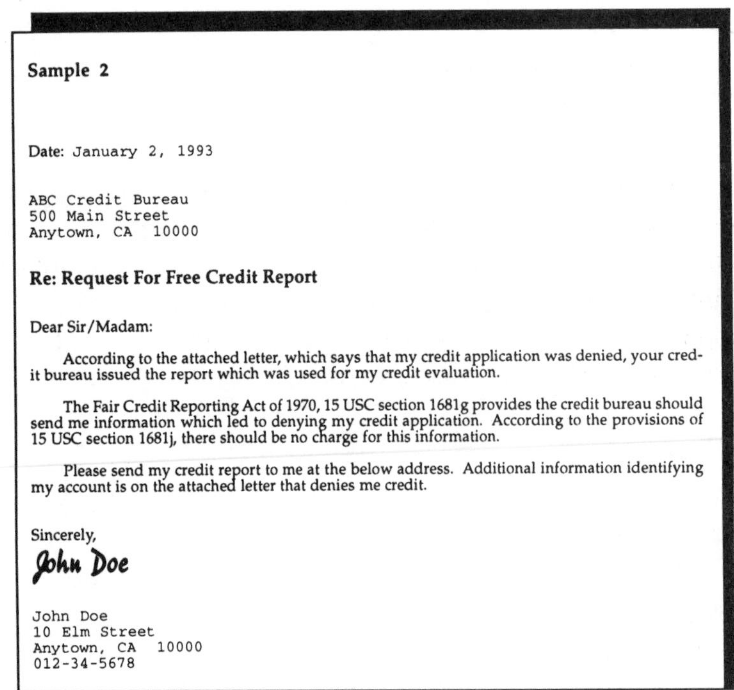

Sample 2

Date: January 2, 1993

ABC Credit Bureau
500 Main Street
Anytown, CA 10000

Re: Request For Free Credit Report

Dear Sir/Madam:

According to the attached letter, which says that my credit application was denied, your credit bureau issued the report which was used for my credit evaluation.

The Fair Credit Reporting Act of 1970, 15 USC section 1681g provides the credit bureau should send me information which led to denying my credit application. According to the provisions of 15 USC section 1681j, there should be no charge for this information.

Please send my credit report to me at the below address. Additional information identifying my account is on the attached letter that denies me credit.

Sincerely,

John Doe

John Doe
10 Elm Street
Anytown, CA 10000
012-34-5678

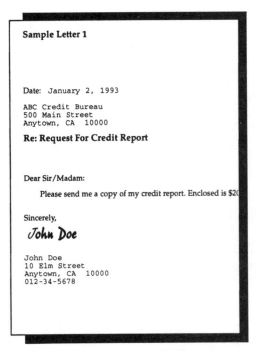

CHAPTER

The 10-step strategy to repairing your credit

With your credit report in hand, you are now ready to repair your credit rating.

The first step is to know your legal rights. What can you do if your credit report contains false, misleading or incomplete information?

The Fair Credit Reporting Act (FCRA), 15 USC sections 1681a through 1681t, protects you against credit abuse that might result in an unfair description of your creditworthiness. Knowing the following six basic rights is essential if you are to successfully erase the negative marks in your credit report and regain a good credit status:

Right #1. You are allowed to challenge the accuracy of your credit report at any time.

Right #2. The credit bureau must reinvestigate anything you challenge.

Right #3. The credit bureau must reinvestigate within a reasonable period of time. The Federal Trade Commission defines reasonable as immediately unless there is some good reason for the delay. For example, a delay might be caused by the large volume of inquiries to the bureau at a particular time.

Right #4. If the credit bureau finds any error, it must promptly delete that erroneous information from its files.

Right #5. If the bureau cannot or does not confirm the information you have challenged within a reasonable time period, it also must delete that information from your files.

Right #6. If a creditor verifies the information and the bureau responds in a timely manner, the negative marks must remain on your record. But if you maintain that the information reported is in dispute, you have the right to submit a Consumer Statement of your view of the problem. In other words, if you as a credit consumer dispute the accuracy of certain information in your report and receive no satisfaction from the bureau or the creditor, then the credit bureau is required by law to attach your explanation to every copy of the report it sends out. You may ask the credit bureau for assistance, but in that case the bureau can limit the statement to 100 words.

You've got right on your side. Now get to work on this 10-step plan.

10-step plan

Highlight

Find the negative remarks, or "dings," in your credit file and circle them.

Step 1. Identify your credit problems.

Find the negative remarks, or "dings," in your credit file and circle them. The information on these reports is usually coded like your bank statement. However, the FCRA requires credit bureaus to explain anything on the report that you cannot reasonably understand. Each report contains a key to the coding symbols. Familiarize yourself with the symbols, then look for damaging remarks in these four sections of your report:

A) The ***Historical Status*** is a record of your monthly payments. Ideally, this should be free of past-due symbols, which may be 30-, 60- or 90-day periods. Almost 90 percent of the bad marks can be from past-due symbols. These could have been entered accidentally, or because the mail was late, or because of delays in processing your payments. Of course, you may have made late payments; you must have your payments credited to your accounts before the due date, not just mailed by that time, if you are to avoid late payment marks.

B) The ***Comments*** section may contain remarks such as Charged to P&L (profit and loss). That means a company has charged an account off as a bad debt loss, and that it does not expect to collect. This, of course, implies that you are a bad credit risk.

C) ***Inquiries*** made by any bank, store or other company to which you applied for credit will be listed in the report. Too many of these may be taken by a potential creditor as an indication that you are in financial difficulty and may be seeking credit as a solution. Creditors will refuse to give credit on the basis of too many inquiries. How many is too many is a subjective judgment by the individual creditor. As few as four or five in six months may be too many for some creditors.

D) ***Public Records*** may appear in your credit report as tax liens, bankruptcies, or court judgments that affected you. These entries should also be examined for accuracy.

Step 2. Determine your overall credit score.

Somewhere on your credit report you will find a column with a title such as Account Profile. This column contains a summary rating for each of your accounts. A summary may read positive, negative, or non-rated. Positive means you are OK; your payments are all on time. Negative means you have a serious credit problem; perhaps you have defaulted on a debt. Non-rated may mean you have a few late payments here and there. Non-rated entries still put you in a weak position, even though there is nothing strongly negative against you. Each negative or non-rated entry has a code reflecting the nature of the problem. Your goal is to protest, and eventually remove, all negative or non-rated profiles.

Highlight

The credit bureau will only verify the facts if you assert that they are in error.

Step 3. Draft a protest to the credit bureau disputing each ding.

To exercise your legal rights, you must aggressively challenge any bad marks or dings. The credit bureau will only verify the facts if you assert that they are in error. So don't be shy. Draft a strong but polite protest for each item you want to challenge, and tell the credit bureau you are exercising your rights under the FCRA, 15 USC section 1681i.

For example, suppose you find the code Charge Off. This means that the creditor charged your account off to profit and loss and that the creditor thinks your debt is uncollectible. You could protest that this comment should be removed because, in fact, the debt was satisfied and therefore should not be reported as a Charge Off. Or perhaps you later paid off the delinquent account, but the creditor failed to note this in your credit report.

Another problem might be a series of Past Due notations. You could protest that those payments were delayed due to a mix-up with the post office when you changed address. Most often the credit bureau and creditor will state that the payment was in fact late, and therefore it is correctly reported. However, if a post office mix-up occurred, you could submit a consumer statement to the effect that the account is in dispute because bills were not delivered by the creditor even though a change of address was furnished.

Step 4. Send your letter of dispute.

Using the sample letters included in this chapter, write a letter of dispute to the credit bureau. Carefully list each ding that you want to challenge. Be sure to include photocopies of any documents that support your claims. These might include correspondence with your creditors, canceled checks indicating payment, receipts, or other documents. Remember that the law states that you have the right to dispute any citation on your report if the information contained in that citation is inaccurate or incomplete (Fair Credit Reporting Act 15 USC section 1681). The only limitation to your dispute is that it should not be frivolous or irrelevant.

When you have finished your letter, make a copy for your records. Send your letter certified mail with return receipt requested to be sure the bureau receives it. It is also a good idea to include a copy of your credit report to make sure the bureau checks the right file. Use Form 3.

Sample 3

Date: January 2, 1993

ABC Credit Bureau
500 Main Street
Anytown, CA 10000

Re: Complaint Letter to Delete Information

Dear Sir/Madam:

I received a copy of my credit report and find the following items to be in error. See the attached copy of the credit report, with these item numbers written next to the problem entries. (Describe)

Item 7 This account was paid on time
Item 14 This was not my obligation to pay

By the provisions of 15 USC section 1681i of the Fair Credit Reporting Act of 1970, I demand that these items be reinvestigated and deleted from my record. Send me names and addresses of individuals you contacted so I may follow up.

I shall assume that 30 days constitutes "reasonable time" for reverification of these entries unless you immediately notify me otherwise. It should be understood that failure to reverify these items within 30 days constitutes reason to promptly drop the information from my file according to Section 1681(a).

Also, pursuant to 15 USC section 1681i (d) of the Fair Credit Reporting Act, please notify me when the items have been deleted. You may send an updated copy of my credit report to the below address. According to the provisions of 15 USC section 1681j, there should be no charge for this notification.

Sincerely,

John Doe

John Doe
10 Elm Street
Anytown, CA 10000
012-34-5678

Form 4 can be used when you wish to merge inquiry with the account. This helps eliminate excessive inquiries from your credit history.

Sample 4

Date: January 2, 1993

ABC Credit Bureau
500 Main Street
Anytown, CA 10000

Re: Request to Merge Inquiry With Account

Dear Sir/Madam:

I recently received my credit report and located problems of inaccurate reporting. A copy of the credit report is attached, with the item numbers marked on the report.

The presence of the inquiries as entries separate from the resulting accounts inaccurately duplicates information. The inquiries reflect an incomplete and inaccurate processing of information in my file. The inquiry entries should be removed, or at least merged into the accounts to which they belong.

Under the provisions of the Fair Credit Reporting Act 15 USC section 1681i, please reinvestigate and delete these disputed items. Send me names and addresses of persons contacted. I shall assume that 30 days constitutes a "reasonable time" to complete these actions unless you immediately notify me otherwise. It should be understood that failure to reverify within this time constitutes non-verification, and the items must be promptly deleted according to Section 1681i (a).

Also, pursuant to 15 USC section 1681i (d) of the Fair Credit Reporting Act, please notify me when the items have been deleted. Send an updated copy of my credit report to the below address. According to 15 USC section 1681j, there is no charge for notification of changes on my credit report.

Sincerely,

John Doe

John Doe
10 Elm Street
Anytown, CA 10000
012-34-5678

Form 5 can be used when incorrect information is on file against you.

Sample 5

Date: January 2, 1993

ABC Credit Bureau
500 Main Street
Anytown, CA 10000

Re: Request to Delete Accounts

Dear Sir/Madam:

I recently received my credit report and located problems of inaccurate reporting. A copy of the credit report is attached, with the item numbers marked in pen on the report.

Under the provisions of the Fair Credit Reporting Act 15 USC section 1681i (a), please reinvestigate and delete these disputed items. Send me names and addresses of persons contacted. I shall assume that 30 days constitutes a "reasonable time" to complete these actions unless you immediately notify me otherwise. It should be understood that failure to reverify within this time constitutes non-verification, and these items must be promptly deleted according to Section 1681i (a).

Also, according to 15 USC section 1681i (d) of the Fair Credit Reporting Act, please send me notification that the items have been deleted. Send an updated copy of my credit report to the below address. According to the provisions of 15 USC section 1681j, there should be no charge for notification of changes on my credit report.

Sincerely,

John Doe

John Doe
10 Elm Street
Anytown, CA 10000
012-34-5678

Form 6 can be used to demand an update of your account, deleting dated comments.

Sample Letter 6

Date: January 2, 1993

ABC Credit Bureau
500 Main Street
Anytown, CA 10000

Re: Request to Update Account

Dear Sir/Madam:

I recently received my credit report and located problems of inaccurate reporting. A copy of the credit report is attached, with the item numbers marked in pen on the report.

Under the provisions of the Fair Credit Reporting Act S15 USC section 1681i, please reinvestigate these disputed items. I shall assume that 30 days constitutes a "reasonable time" to complete these actions unless you immediately notify me otherwise. It should be understood that failure to reverify within this time constitutes non-verification, and the items must be promptly deleted according to 15 USC section 1681i (a).

Also, pursuant to 15 USc section 1681i (d) of the Fair Credit Reporting Act, please send me notification that the items have been deleted. Send an updated copy of my credit report to the below address. According to the provisions of 15 USC section 1681j, there should be no charge for notification of changes on my credit report.

Sincerely,

John Doe

John Doe
10 Elm Street
Anytown, CA 10000
012-34-5678

Step 5. Record your actions.

As soon as you mail the letter, log the date for each ding or negative entry you have protested. Keep related disputes together in a file with copies of the letter, the credit report, and any other documents you include.

Step 6. Wait a reasonable time for a response.

The waiting period will depend on several factors. Mark on your calendar the date when you figure a reasonable time has elapsed. You should not tolerate a delay longer than eight weeks.

Step 7. Send follow-up letters.

If the credit bureau does not respond within a reasonable time, write follow-up letters. Point out that federal law requires the credit bureau to respond to a consumer dispute within a reasonable period of time or the agency is in default. Use Form 7 as the first reminder. This will be sufficient to prompt a response from most credit bureaus.

Sample 7

Date: January 2, 1993

ABC Credit Bureau
500 Main Street
Anytown, CA 10000

Re: Reminder to Respond

Dear Sir/Madam:

Thirty days ago you received my letter disputing several items listed in my credit report, issued by your firm. The items were inaccurate and incomplete. I have attached the original letter.

Note that 30 days is considered a "reasonable time" under the Fair Credit Reporting Act, 15 USC section 1681i for responding to my request for reverification of the erroneous items. Since you did not immediately write to inform me of the need for additional time, I presume you accepted the 30 day time limit.

I have not received a reply from you within this 30 days. Therefore, it must be that the information on my report was either inaccurate, or it could not be reverified. In either case, according to the provisions of 15 USC section 1681i (a) the items must be deleted immediately.

Please respond immediately so that I do not need to pursue my legal rights under 15 USC section 1681n or 1681o, which require your compliance to the law.

Also, pursuant to 15 USC section 1681i (d) of the Fair Credit Reporting Act, please send me notification that the items have been deleted. Send an updated copy of my credit report to the below address, as well as to any other party that has inquired about my credit rating in the last six months. According to the provisions of 15 USC section 1681j, there should be no charge for notification of changes on my credit report.

Sincerely,

John Doe

John Doe
10 Elm Street
Anytown, CA 10000
012-34-5678

Should the credit bureau fail to respond within 30 days of the reminder, use Form 8 as the final follow-up.

Sample 8

Date: January 2, 1993

ABC Credit Bureau
500 Main Street
Anytown, CA 10000

Re: Final Follow-Up on Failure to Respond

Dear Sir/Madam:

On November 1, 1992, I sent you a follow-up letter pointing out that you had failed to respond to my disputes of certain items found on my credit report, issued by your company. Copies of that letter and the original dispute letter are attached.

To date you still have not fulfilled the intent and letter of the Fair Credit Reporting Act, which requires your bureau, as a consumer reporting agency, to maintain and ensure that information "is fair and equitable to the consumer."

Also, the law stipulates that bureaus will maintain "accuracy, relevancy, and proper utilization of such information" (15 USC section 1681e).

These requirements have not been met by your actions. You have not given me evidence that you have acted in a prompt or "fair and equitable" manner.

1) You have not submitted evidence of investigation by giving me names and addresses of persons contacted, nor have you removed anything found inaccurate.

2) You have not removed any item for which no verification could be found within the 30 days' "reasonable time."

3) You have not taken care to maintain the accuracy, relevancy, and proper use of information in my file.

I still dispute the items given on my attached letter. I expect an appropriate response on or before March 1, 1993, for each item. Otherwise I must contact the Federal Trade Commission.

I also expect the names and addresses of individuals you contacted to verify the information so I may follow up on any item.

Sincerely,

John Doe

John Doe
10 Elm Street
Anytown, CA 10000
012-34-5678

In the event the credit bureau ignores both the initial reminder and final follow-up, send Form 9. Failure of the credit bureau to respond in a timely manner entitles you to have deleted any negative mark on your report that you challenged.

Sample 9

Date: January 2, 1993

ABC Credit Bureau
500 Main Street
Anytown, CA 10000

Re: Demand For Corrected Credit Report

Dear Sir/Madam:

On November 1, 1992, I wrote to tell you I had not heard about any specific actions taken to reverify the items I had identified as inaccurate or incomplete in my credit report. Copies of my correspondence are attached for your review.

Since you have not given me names of persons you contacted for reverification of the information nor have you complied within a "reasonable time" to my request for reverification, I assume that you have not been able to reverify the information I have disputed. Therefore, you must comply with the provision of the Fair Credit Reporting Act, and drop the disputed items from my credit report.

I demand that you send me a copy of my updated credit report showing the elimination of the items which I disputed on the attached letters. This copy must be provided free, according to 15 USC section 1681j. I demand that it be postmarked within five days after signing the certified mail receipt for the letter you are holding.

If I do not receive an updated copy of my credit report, with the disputed items dropped, my attorney will pursue my legal rights under 15 USC section 1681n or 1681o of the Fair Credit Reporting Act, "Civil liability for willful noncompliance." Your credit bureau may be liable for:

1) Any actual damages I sustain by your failure to delete the items;
2) Punitive damages as the court may allow; and
3) Costs of the court action, plus attorney's fees.

I have forwarded a copy of this letter to the Federal Trade Commission.

Sincerely,

John Doe

John Doe
10 Elm Street
Anytown, CA 10000
012-34-5678

If the credit bureau fails to provide an immediate updated credit report, free of the disputed entry, you have several methods of recourse:

1) The Federal Trade Commission can bring legal action against the bureau.
2) The bureau can be liable to you for damages resulting from further issuance of the old report.
3) The bureau can also be liable for your attorney fees.

Highlight

It is frequently possible to eliminate negative marks simply by going through this process of disputing entries.

It is frequently possible to eliminate negative marks simply by going through this process of disputing entries. Since many creditors won't take the time or make the effort to defend the negative entry, you can eventually repair your credit through the default of your creditors.

Step 8. Ask for an updated credit report.

At the end of your letters are requests for an updated copy of your credit report. 15 USC section 1681j of the FCRA requires the bureau to send a free notification of any updates to anyone who has received a copy of the report within six months previous to any corrections or statements that are added to the report. Therefore, you are entitled to receive a free update. When you request it, include a request to send an update to anyone else who has recently inquired about your credit.

Note: The bureaus are not required to send a copy of the entire report, but they will often do so because that is more convenient for them.

Step 9. Compare the new report with the prior report.

Most bureaus send you an updated report. Compare carefully the updated report with the original one. Mark with a star any negative entry that has moved up to non-rated, or any non-rated or negative entry that has moved up to positive. Chances are that you will not get results on every protest the first time, but some progress is likely. Notice that the bureau may delete some items only because a creditor failed to respond to its investigation in a timely manner. This commonly occurs: The creditor's failure to deal with a bothersome piece of paperwork has now been turned to your advantage and is helping to clear your record.

Step 10. Repeat the process.

There are probably still some bad marks remaining. Also, it sometimes happens that a dispute results in an update to an account that is even more negative than before. For example, reinvestigation could uncover the fact that you actually had more late payments than were previously reported.

So what do you do? Now it is time to go back to the beginning of the process and start over again. You should put your credit record through this process at least twice before going on to the next phase. Remember that credit cannot be rebuilt in a day. It takes patience and persistence. Also remember that during this process you must be very careful not to allow any new problems to appear on your record. Keep all your accounts current or pay ahead of schedule.

Highlight

Remember that credit cannot be rebuilt in a day. It takes patience and persistence.

CHAPTER

Gain creditor cooperation

Many negative remarks cannot be deleted without creditor cooperation because the dings are accurate and the creditor persistently cooperates with the bureau's request for verification. Your goal then is to persuade your creditors to soften their stance by either toning down or entirely deleting their remarks on your credit report. In the next stage we will get more creative and attempt to persuade the creditor to remove the damaging remarks completely. But for now we only want to turn those current bad debts into positive credit ratings. Here are eight steps to follow:

Step 1. Set up a worksheet for each creditor

Accurate record keeping is an essential part of your dealings with the creditors who still give you bad marks. Use a creditor worksheet containing names, account numbers, credit remarks, and any documents, correspondence or notes you have on your dealings with them.

Step 2. Write to each creditor

After studying all the facts concerning each account and the nature of the credit complaints, write each creditor explaining your version of how the problem arose. Use Sample Letter 10 as a guide, but don't be afraid to expand upon it. Be specific and give all the relevant details, including full documentation. Be factual, but appeal to the creditor's sense of goodwill. Perhaps your company went bankrupt suddenly, or you lost your job. Or perhaps you were detained several weeks in a foreign country while on a business trip and therefore unable to pay your accounts on time. Remind the creditor that you eventually paid, and mention that you appreciated his or her services and products in spite of the payment problems that arose. Appeal to the creditor's compassion; ask that the bad marks be removed now that the account is settled, or ask that the creditor put a statement into your credit report stating that the account is paid up.

As you write the letter, consider it in light of your other accounts that may have been affected by the same circumstances. Each letter you send should be consistent with the others so that, if your creditors' new comments appear on your credit file, they will appear reasonable and consistent. Don't send in weak excuses for late bill-paying habits. Use strong, compelling reasons. Send the letter by certified mail, return receipt requested. To help document the process, keep a copy of each letter and receipt with your worksheet file.

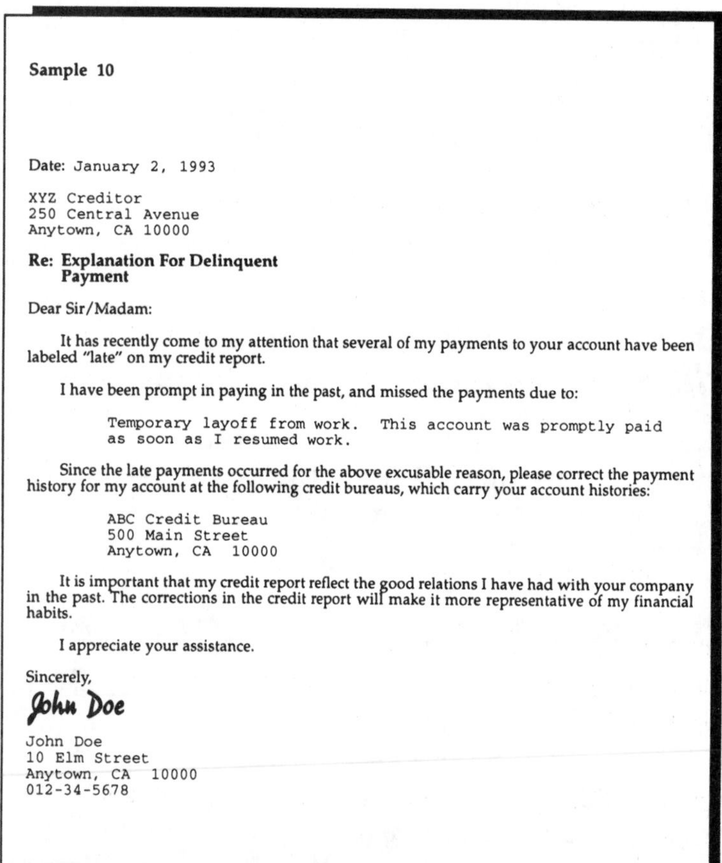

Sample 10

Date: January 2, 1993

XYZ Creditor
250 Central Avenue
Anytown, CA 10000

Re: Explanation For Delinquent Payment

Dear Sir/Madam:

It has recently come to my attention that several of my payments to your account have been labeled "late" on my credit report.

I have been prompt in paying in the past, and missed the payments due to:

Temporary layoff from work. This account was promptly paid as soon as I resumed work.

Since the late payments occurred for the above excusable reason, please correct the payment history for my account at the following credit bureaus, which carry your account histories:

ABC Credit Bureau
500 Main Street
Anytown, CA 10000

It is important that my credit report reflect the good relations I have had with your company in the past. The corrections in the credit report will make it more representative of my financial habits.

I appreciate your assistance.

Sincerely,

John Doe

John Doe
10 Elm Street
Anytown, CA 10000
012-34-5678

Step 3. Order an updated credit report after 30 days

Your letters may convince your creditors to cooperate and remove dings. Allow about 30 days for the creditor to respond, and then order a new credit report to see if the creditor has made any changes in your report. Have the remaining bad marks been deleted? Have some softer remarks been added?

Highlight

Don't be bashful or discouraged. Try again. Be persistent. Talk to a different person.

Step 4. Contact the creditor by telephone

If letters are futile, use the telephone. This will allow you to interact with the creditor in a more personal way. Before you call, study the information you have gathered from your credit report, your creditors' responses, and the worksheet you have compiled. Then write a simple outline of all the points that you want to make during your call.

Step 5. Be persistent

Sometimes the first call to a creditor will have no effect. Don't be bashful or discouraged. Try again. Be persistent. Talk to a different person. Large companies will have many people working in their customer relations departments. Each person will react differently to you, and sooner or later you may find someone who will relate more positively to your problem.

Once a creditor agrees that a change in your report is justified, ask on the phone that the change be made in your credit status. Offer to send the creditor a letter with that agreement in writing, along with a self-addressed, stamped envelope. (Be certain to obtain the creditor's name and office address.) The creditor should sign the letter and return it to you for your own records. This letter is important if the creditor forgets to change your status or later changes his or her mind about helping you. You can send this letter to the credit agency yourself to repair your credit.

Step 6. Send your statement to the credit bureau

If the creditor has not improved the marks on your report, you should write directly to the bureau and ask it to add your consumer statement to the account in accordance with 15 USC section 1681i (b) of the FCRA. Your comments as to why the bill was not paid on time will then be submitted with your credit report in response to any credit request. Your comments may greatly mitigate the damage of a particular entry. Sample 11 shows you how it might be done.

Sample 11

Date: January 2, 1993

ABC Credit Bureau
500 Main Street
Anytown, CA 10000

Re: Consumer Statement

Dear Sir/Madam:

According to the Fair Credit Reporting Act 15 USC section 1611i (b), I have the right to enter a "consumer statement" in my credit report. I have disputed the accuracy and completeness of the items circled in pen on the attached credit report.

Since reinvestigation has not resolved my dispute, I want the following statement included in my credit report to set forth the nature of my dispute for others to see.

> That payment to Acme Co. was not made because goods were delivered in a defective condition and Acme refused to repair or replace said items.

According to the Fair Credit Reporting Act, please send me a free updated copy of my credit report with the above statement included.

I assume that 30 days represents a "reasonable time" for completing this update, unless you immediately notify me.

Sincerely,

John Doe

John Doe
10 Elm Street
Anytown, CA 10000
012-34-5678

Highlight

Don't be bashful or discouraged. Try again. Be persistent. Talk to a different person.

You may not want to comment on any one particular entry, but want your credit record to reflect reasons for a generally poor report. For example, if you have several negative entries, were they caused by:

- A layoff from work?
- Divorce?
- Personal or family illness?
- Tax problems?

Highlight

Point out your prior track record. Be convincing that these problems are behind you and are not likely to recur.

You see the idea. These unfortunate experiences can hit anyone and wreak havoc on an excellent credit history. Let credit inquiries know if there was one definable event that ruined your good credit. Point out your prior track record. Be convincing that these problems are behind you and are not likely to recur. Sample 12 can be used to ensure that such a consumer statement is added to your credit record.

Sample 12

Date: January 2, 1993

ABC Credit Bureau
500 Main Street
Anytown, CA 10000

Re: Request For Addition of Supplementary Credit History Information

Dear Sir/Madam:

Please include in my credit report the supplemental information attached.

According to the Fair Credit Reporting Act (FCRA), 15 USC section 1681b, "It is the purpose of this title (FCRA) to require that consumer reporting agencies adopt reasonable procedures for meeting the needs of commerce for consumer credit, personnel, insurance, and other information in a manner which is fair and equitable to the consumer, with regard to the confidentiality, accuracy, relevancy, and proper utilization of such information in accordance with the requirements of this title." The intent of the FCRA includes recording supplementary credit information if requested by a consumer.

Accordingly, I hereby request that you add the attached history of payments, under the FCRA, 15 USC section 1681i.

Thank you for your attention. Please inform me within 30 days of your compliance with the 15 USC section 1681e requirements that a consumer's credit report should reflect "completeness and accuracy" within a "reasonable" time after notification by the consumer.

Sincerely,

John Doe

John Doe
10 Elm Street
Anytown, CA 10000
012-34-5678

Step 7. Wait the estimated time for a reply

Now the ball is again with the bureau. You must wait the estimated time that you established when you initially persuaded the bureau to remove the dings. In a few weeks the bureau should reply and may also send you an updated copy of your report. If your statement appears positive, you may be ready to start using your credit again.

Step 8. Try again

Remember persistence. Wait a few months and repeat the process. After the lapse of time the situation may have changed. See what happens when you try the creditor again. After a few months have gone by you may find a new person in the office who will be more cooperative and willing to help you regain a good credit rating.

Highlight

Remember persistence. Wait a few months and repeat the process.

CHAPTER

How to turn current financial problems into a positive rating

Did you know you can successfully turn even current bad debts into a positive credit rating? Your goal is to approach these creditors and negotiate repayment plans that sincerely demonstrate your ability to make regular payments on time, pay off the debts you owe, and revive their interest in you as a customer. In return you are going to ask your creditors to restore your positive credit rating.

How can this be accomplished if your account has gone to a collection agency? If this has happened, deal first with the original creditor. A collection agency receives a percentage of what it collects from you, so it will try to get as much cash as possible from you. The creditor, on the other hand, may have already given up any expectation of full payment. By dealing with the creditor, you may have more flexibility to negotiate the time or the amount to pay.

Often, because of his agreement with the collection agency, the creditor may not deal with you after turning over your account for collection. Remember, the collection agency is not consumer-oriented and will be more difficult to negotiate with. Therefore, it's always best to do what you can to avoid having a debt turned over for collection. If you cannot avoid negotiating with the collection agency, use the following pointers, which also apply to dealing with a creditor.

1) Make a win-win offer to the creditor.

Keep in mind that your goal is to trade money for a positive credit rating on your credit report. Perhaps you can offer to set up a payment schedule in exchange for a promise to improve your payment history. For example, you could agree to pay 100 percent of what you owe in 12 monthly installments in exchange for the creditor agreeing to recognize your new bill-paying commitment with better credit ratings. Let's be even more specific: Perhaps you can agree that after three months of punctual payments, a negative rating could be raised to a non-rating. Perhaps after six months of regular payments, the non-rating could be lifted to a positive rating. You see the idea.

2) Obtain open account status.

It looks bad when your account is closed to further purchases, even if you are making regular payments. Therefore, when you are negotiating an offer, ask to reopen your account while you uphold your end of the agreement. You can be very persuasive if you offer to pay 100 percent of the debt, perhaps with some interest or a service charge added. If the creditor will give you a clean bill of credit health, your extra effort to pay him is certainly worth it. Caution: Make sure the terms you finally agree upon are within the range of your budget so you can faithfully keep your promise.

Highlight

Carefully repeat all the points of agreement over the phone to get the creditor's verification. Then type up the agreement as a letter, sign it, and send it to the creditor with a stamped, self-addressed envelope.

3) Put it in writing.

The win-win negotiation procedure up to this point can be carried out over the telephone. However, once you have reached verbal agreement it is vital to put it in writing. Carefully repeat all the points of agreement over the phone to get the creditor's verification. Then type up the agreement as a letter, sign it, and send it to the creditor with a stamped, self-addressed envelope. Before you send the letter, however, you may want your lawyer to check the wording. Once the creditor signs the agreement and returns it to you, it can become part of your credit record.

4) Honor the agreement.

Now that you have a written agreement, you need only fulfill it and your credit rating will be restored. So be punctual. Make every payment on or ahead of time. Be responsible. If your ability to meet the payment schedule in the agreement should be threatened by unemployment or illness, inform your creditor right away, before you miss any payments. Let your creditors know your plans for meeting the payments, and explore ways to solve your temporary setback that will meet everyone's needs.

5) Verify your credit upgrade.

Before using your newly improved credit status, remember to order an updated copy of your credit file to verify that the creditor has honored his or her side of the agreement and made the promised changes. Allow a reasonable time period from the date the creditor agreed to make the changes, and then request your update. If the changes have not been made, call the person who made the agreement and remind that person of his or her side of the agreement.

If the agreed changes are not made, you can dispute the information on your credit report. Use a copy of the creditor-signed agreement (see Point 3) as supporting evidence for the change.

Tax liens and your credit rating

Highlight

To ensure that you obtain a Certificate of Release for each lien filed, you must conduct a complete lien search. This can be done in several ways.

A tax lien on your credit report will definitely hurt your chances for a loan to buy a home, business, car, boat or any other major purchase. It may also prevent you from obtaining credit cards.

Unfortunately, the fact that you had tax liens may not be erased from your credit report until the taxes have been paid for seven years. However, a past lien isn't nearly as damaging as a current tax lien. That's why you must be certain every credit bureau updates your credit history to show that your outstanding tax liens have been fully paid and discharged.

Once you have fully paid your taxes, the IRS must send you a Certificate of Release of Federal Tax Lien (Form 668Z). You must receive a certificate for each office that has a lien on file. This may include the clerk of your city, town or county, the Federal District Court nearest where you reside, and wherever real estate transactions for your locale are recorded. If you have moved, there may be liens filed where you originally lived. There may also be several liens for the same tax liability filed in the same place. This commonly occurs if your tax problems extend over a number of years. To ensure that you obtain a Certificate of Release for each lien filed, you must conduct a complete lien search. This can be done in several ways:

1) Ask the IRS agent for copies of every lien the IRS has filed against you.

2) Have a commercial lien search service comb the public records. These firms know how and where to look for liens, but be certain they know everywhere you lived or worked from the very beginning of your tax troubles. Also let them know of any change of name. One reputable company is Docu-Search. The toll-free number is (800) 332-3034. The company gives good, reliable nationwide service at a reasonable cost; however, there are many other excellent firms that provide the same service.

3) Review your credit report. This may disclose outstanding tax liens, but don't rely upon your credit report alone. A credit report may easily overlook some tax liens.

4) Conduct your own lien search. It's very simple. The clerk at the public recording office is usually cooperative and will assist you in your search.

Once you are satisfied you have identified all the recorded liens, make certain the IRS files a Certificate of Release for each lien. Don't assume the IRS will do this on its own. Frequently it doesn't. You must be diligent in following up on this or you'll have outstanding tax liens that will haunt you for years. Remember: One outstanding tax lien can ruin your chances for credit.

Review your credit reports. For each recorded lien that is not noted as discharged, you must insist that the reporting agency contact the IRS or check the public records to confirm that the lien has been released. You may also send the credit bureaus copies of the Certificate of Release of Federal Tax Lien. Follow up to make sure your credit report reflects the discharge of all tax liens against you.

Highlight

For each recorded lien that is not noted as discharged, you must insist that the reporting agency contact the IRS or check the public records to confirm that the lien has been released.

Credit bureaus can be slow to update your credit report. You can be penalized with poor credit for many years only because the credit bureaus stubbornly show outstanding liens. So it is up to you to clear your credit profile and rebuild your credit.

You can even help your credit picture if you are only now resolving your tax problems. For example, if you pay the IRS in installments, then your credit report can reflect the anticipated discharge of your lien because an agreement has been reached with the IRS. You can submit a statement to the credit bureau and insist that it accompany your credit report.

It is possible to erase existing (and unpaid) tax liens by following the same strategies used for erasing other negatives. If you challenge a tax lien, the government does not always substantiate the lien within the required 30 days. In many instances, the government won't respond to the credit bureau for 45 to 60 days. Nevertheless, since the documentation was not provided within the required 30 days, the credit bureau must delete the tax lien notice and cannot later reinstate it. You will be most successful if you attempt to erase the tax lien after your tax file has been transferred to the governmental archives. This transfer usually takes about a year. Having your tax file in the archives often increases the turnaround time to retrieve the records beyond the required 30 days.

Bankruptcy, repossession, foreclosure

We have shown you how to clear up the majority of things that can occur in a credit report. However, you may have encountered some serious problems in your financial past, such as bankruptcies, court claims, repossessions, or foreclosures. These negatives may stick to your credit report after you try every method we discussed. For these major problems we can only recommend the virtues of patience and persistence. You will be surprised at how much you can accomplish merely by sticking it out. As these events drift further into your past, they will become less significant in your credit history.

Highlight

You cannot be penalized forever for past mistakes.

You should know, however, that any adverse information more than seven years old must be deleted from your file, whether it is challenged or not. You cannot be penalized forever for past mistakes. One exception to this is a bankruptcy, which may be kept on your record up to 10 years. Another exception is that if you request credit or life insurance worth $50,000 or more, or apply for a job paying $20,000 or more, the credit bureau may release an unexpurgated version of your credit history. This otherwise-deleted information is kept in a separate file that can only be released in the above-mentioned circumstances.

How credit clinics can ease bad credit

Through vigorous application of the Fair Credit Reporting Act (FCRA), many entrepreneurs have opened businesses that claim the ability to clear your credit record. The strategy these clinics use generally works, clearing most of the negative items (true or not) from your credit profile years before they would have been eliminated under the time limits set by federal law. However, applying their strategy of credit repair is so simple that you do not need a credit clinic to help you. It can be done on your own.

How do these credit clinics operate? First, they know what credit bureaus will not tell you: that each item on a record must be proven if it is to remain. If the bureau cannot prove the item, it must be removed from the file regardless of whether it is true. The clinics also know that every negative entry can be denied or challenged at any time. The bureau must then reinvestigate. If the item cannot be reverified within a reasonable period of time, it is automatically removed from the file. Most bureaus give themselves 20 or so working days to reverify.

The clinic will have you send a letter to the credit bureau denying all of the negative items in your file. You will state that the negative items are incorrect, or that it isn't your account, or that you don't recall making a late payment. The letter is sent to the bureau with a demand for reinvestigation of the disputed items. About a month later you will receive a corrected report that likely has some of the negative items removed.

How were these blotches removed? There are several things that can force the credit bureau to erase the items. It may run up against the time limit for reverification. It could have been very busy and not had the time to handle it properly. There's also a small chance that a negative item will be mistakenly erased. Operators do make errors.

When the credit bureau contacts the original source of the data to verify account information, sometimes the creditor does not verify or fails to do so within the time limit. Some creditors do not bother to respond to reverification because it is extra work for them. If you have had trouble with an account in the past but it is corrected now, the creditor may not care to continue punishing you, and eventually may give up on reverification. Please note that if you are currently in controversy with a creditor, that creditor will almost always make a strong effort to keep the negative item on your record. However, the urge to keep it on diminishes once the problem has been rectified.

Highlight

Please note that if you are currently in controversy with a creditor, that creditor will almost always make a strong effort to keep the negative item on your record.

In addition, many creditors keep account information for only two or three years. So if you challenge an item that old, it is possible that it cannot be verified, since the records no longer exist.

Credit clinics also understand the value of persistence. After one to six months, the credit clinic will have you send another letter to the bureau, starting the process all over again. And the clinics usually encourage you to continue this until all of your negative items are removed. Should you tire of this at any point, the clinic will have you add a consumer statement counteracting any negative items that may be remaining on your credit profile.

You don't need to pay a credit clinic to repair your credit. With the *E-Z Legal Guide to Credit Repair* you can easily and inexpensively do it on your own.

Bolster your credit record

What about all of those positive accounts you have that aren't listed on your credit report? Do you have sterling payment records that are unmentioned? If so, you can have these placed on your report.

The law remains unclear about adding favorable items to a credit report, but the FTC has advised credit bureaus that where a report has resulted in unfavorable action against a debtor, the debtor should be able to add to the report to create a more complete and balanced picture of his or her repayment history. Consequently, most credit bureaus will, for a small fee, contact any creditor you name and add that creditor's favorable information to your file. The charge will usually be $2 to $3 per item.

If you feel it will help in offsetting some negative items on your report, or that it will fill out an otherwise incomplete report, adding a creditor's favorable information is well worth the investment.

Highlight

Most credit bureaus will, for a small fee, contact any creditor you name and add that creditor's favorable information to your file. The charge will usually be $2 to $3 per item.

Call your non-reporting creditors with whom you have a good relationship and a spotless payment record. Let them know you need your account information listed on your credit report. Once they agree to release your account record, tell them which credit bureau will contact them. Do this for each good account you want listed.

Next, contact the credit bureau with your list of additions. Ask the credit bureau to contact these creditors and add the items to your report as soon as the information is verified.

Once you have cleared your credit report of as many negative items as possible and added all possible positive items, you should have a new and reasonably good credit report, one that will give you the credit you need for a more enjoyable future.

Credit Repair

The forms in this guide

Request for Credit Report 66
Request for Free Credit Report 67
Complaint Letter to Delete Information 68
Request to Merge Inquiry with Account 69
Request to Delete Accounts 70
Request to Update Account 71
Reminder to Respond 72
Final Follow-up on Failure to Respond 73
Demand for Corrected Credit Report 74
Explanation for Delinquent Payment 75
Consumer Statement 76
Request for Addition of Supplementary Credit History 77

Form 1

Date:
Address:

Re: Request For Credit Report

Dear Sir/Madam:

Please send me a copy of my credit report.
Enclosed is a $____________, as payment for the credit report.

Sincerely,

Name (Printed)
Address, City, State, Zip
Social Security Number

Form 2

Date:
Address:

Re: Request for Free Credit Report

Dear Sir/Madam:

According to the attached letter, which says that my credit application was denied, your credit bureau issued the report which was used for my credit evaluation.

The Fair credit Reporting Act of 1970, 15 USC section 1681g provides the credit bureau should send me information which led to denying my credit application. Accourding to the provisions of 15 USC section 1681j, there should be no charge for this information.

Please send me my credit report to me at the below address. Additional information identilfying mya ccount is ont he attached letter that denies me credit.

Sincerely,

Name (Printed)
Address, City, State, Zip
Social Security Number

Form 3

Date:

Address:

Re: Complaint Letter to Delete Information

Dear Sir/Madam:

I received a copy of my credit report to find the following items to be in error. See the attache dcopy of the credit report, with these item numbers written next to the probelm entries. (Describe)

By the provisions of 15 USC section 1681i of the Fair Credit Reporting Act of 1970, I demmand that these items be reinvestigated and deleted from my record. Send me names and addresses of individuals ou contacted so I mmay follow up.

I shall assume that 30 days consitutes "reasonable time" for reverification of these entries unless you immediately notify me otherwise. It shoudl be understood that fialure to revierfy these items within 30 days constitutes reason to promptly drop the information from my file according to Section 1681i (a).

Also, pursuant to 15 USC section 1681i (d) of the Fair Credit Reporting Act, please notify me when the items have been deleted. You may send an updated copy of my credit report to the below address. According to the provisions of 15 USC section 1681j, there should be no charge for this notification.

Sincerely,

Name (Print)
Address, City, State, Zip
Social Security Number

Form 4

Date:

Address:

Re: Request to Merge Inquiry With Account

Dear Sir/Madam:

I recently received my credit report and located problems of inaccurate reporting. A copy of the credit report is attached, with the item numbers marked on the report.

The presence of the inquiries as entries separate from the resulting accounts inaccurately duplicates information. The inquiries reflect an incomplete and inaccurate processing of information in my file. The inquiry entries should be removed, or at least merged into the accounts to which they belong.

Under the provisions of the Fair Credit Reporting Act 15 USC section 1681i, please reinvestigate and delete these disputed items. Send me names and addresses of persons contacted. I shall assume that 30 days constitutes a "reasonable time" to complete these actions unless you immediately notify me otherwise. It should be understood that failure to reverify within this time constitutes non-verification, and the items must be promptly deleted according to Section 1681i (a).

Also, pursuant to 15 USC section 1681i (d) of the Fair Credit Reporting Act, please notify me when the items have been deleted. Send an updated copy of my credit report to the below address. According to 15 USC section 1681j, there is no charge for notification of changes on my credit report.

Sincerely,

Name (Print)
Address, City, State, Zip
Social Security Number

Form 5

Date:

Address:

Re: Request to Delete Accounts

Dear Sir/Madam:

I recently received my credit report and located problems of inaccurate reporting. A copy of the credit report is attached, with the item numbers marked in pen on the report.

Under the provisions of the Fair Credit Reporting Act 15 USC section 1681i (a), please reinvestigate and delete these disputed items. Send me names and addresses of persons contacted. I shall assume that 30 days constitutes a "reasonable time" to complete these actions unless you immediately notify me otherwise. It should be understood that failure to reverify within this time constitutes non-verification, and these items must be promptly deleted according to Section 1681i (a).

Also, according to 15 USC section 1681i (d) of the Fair Credit Reporting Act, please send me notification that the items have been deleted. Send an updated copy of my credit report to the below address. According to the provisions of 15 USC section 1681j, there should be no charge for notification of changes on my credit report.

Sincerely,

Name (Printed)
Address, City, State, Zip
Social Security Number

Form 6

Date:

Address

Re: Request to Update Account

Dear Sir/Madam:

I recently received my credit report and located problems of inaccurate reporting. A copy of the credit report is attached, with the item numbers marked in pen on the report.

Under the provisions of the Fair Credit Reporting Act S15 USC section 1681i, please reinvestigate these disputed items. I shall assume that 30 days constitutes a "reasonable time" to complete these actions unless you immediately notify me otherwise. It should be understood that failure to reverify within this time constitutes non-verification, and the items must be promptly deleted according to 15 USC section 1681i (a).

Also, pursuant to 15 USc section 1681i (d) of the Fair Credit Reporting Act, please send me notification that the items have been deleted. Send an updated copy of my credit report to the below address. According to the provisions of 15 USC section 1681j, there should be no charge for notification of changes on my credit report.

Sincerely,

Name (Printed)
Address, City, State, Zip
Social Security Number

Form 7

Date:

Address:

Re: Reminder to Respond

Dear Sir/Madam:

Thirty days ago you received my letter disputing several items listed in my credit report, issued by your firm. The items were inaccurate and incomplete. I have attached the original letter.

Note that 30 days is considered a "reasonable time" under the Fair Credit Reporting Act, 15 USC section 1681i for responding to my request for reverification of the erroneous items. Since you did not immediately write to inform me of the need for additional time, I presume you accepted the 30-day time limit.

I have not received a reply from you within this 30 days. Therefore, it must be that the information on my report was either inaccurate, or it could not be reverified. In either case, according to the provisions of 15 USC section 1681i (a), the items must be deleted immediately.

Please respond immediately so that I do not need to pursue my legal rights under 15 USC section 1681n or 1681o, which require your compliance to the law.

Also, pursuant to 15 USC section 1681i (d) of the Fair Credit Reporting Act, please send me notification that the items have been deleted. Send an updated copy of my credit report to the below address, as well as to any other party that has inquired about my credit rating in the last six months. According to the provisions of 15 USC section 1681j, there should be no charge for notification of changes on my credit report.

Sincerely,

Name (Printed)
Address, City, State, Zip
Social Security Number

Form 8

Date:

Address:

Re: Final Follow-up on Failure to Respond

Dear Sir/Madam:

On , 19 , I sent you a follow-up letter pointing out that you had failed to respond to my disputes of certain items found on my credit report, issued by your company. Copies of that letter and the original dispute letter are attached.

To date you still have not fulfilled the intent and letter of the Fair Credit Reporting Act, which requires your bureau, as a consumer reporting agency, to maintain and ensure that information "is fair and equitable to the consumer."

Also, the law stipulates that bureaus will maintain "accuracy, relevancy, and proper utilization of such information" (15 USC section 1681e).

These requirements have not been met by your actions. You have not given me evidence that you have acted in a prompt or "fair and equitable" manner.

1) You have not submitted evidence of investigation by giving me names and addresses of persons contacted, nor have your removed anything found inaccurate.

2) You have not removed any item for which no verification could be found within the 30 days' "reasonable time."

3) You have not taken care to maintain the accuracy, relevancy, and proper use of information in my file.

I still dispute the items given on my attached letter. I expect an appropriate response on or before , for each item. Otherwise I must contact the Federal Trade Commission.

I also expect the names and addresses of individuals you contacted to verify the information so I may follow up on any item.

Sincerely,

Name (Print)
Address, City, State, Zip
Social Security Number

Date:

Address:

Re: Demand For Corrected Credit Report

Dear Sir/Madam:

On , 19 , I wrote to tell you I had not heard about any specific actions taken to reverify the items I had identified as inaccurate or incomplete in my credit report. Copies of my correspondence are attached for your review.

Since you have not given me names of persons you contacted for reverification of the information nor have you complied within a "reasonable time" to my request for reverification, I assume that you have not been able to reverify the information I have disputed. Therefore, you must comply with the provision of the Fair Credit Reporting Act, and drop the disputed items from my credit report.

I demand that you send me a copy of my updated credit report showing the elimination of the items which I disputed on the attached letters. This copy must be provided free, according to 15 USC section 1681j. I demand that it be postmarked within five days after signing the certified mail receipt for the letter you are holding.

If I do not receive an updated copy of my credit report with the disputed items dropped, my attorney will pursue my legal rights under 15 USC section 1681n or 1681o of the Fair Credit Reporting Act, "Civil liability for willful noncompliance." Your credit bureau may be liable for:

1) Any actual damages I sustain by your failure to delete the items;
2) Punitive damages as the court may allow; and
3) Costs of the court action, plus attorney's fees.

I have forwarded a copy of this letter to the Federal Trade Commission.

Sincerely,

Name (Print)
Address, City, State, Zip
Social Security Number

Form 10

Date:

Address:

Re: Explanation For Delinquent Payment

Dear Sir/Madam:

It has recently come to my attention that several of my payments to your account have been labeled "late" on my credit report.

I have been prompt in paying in the past, and missed the payments due to:

Since the late payments occurred for the above excusable reason, please correct the payment history for my account at the following credit bureaus, which carry your account histories:

It is important that my credit report reflect the good relations I have had with your company in the past. The corrections in the credit report will make it more representative of my financial habits.

I appreciate your assistance.

Sincerely,

Name (Print)
Address, City, State, Zip
Social Security Number

Date:

Address:

Re: Consumer Statement

Dear Sir/Madam:

According to the Fair Credit Reporting Act 15 USC section 1611i (b), I have the right to enter a "consumer statement" in my credit report. I have disputed the accuracy and completeness of the items circled in pen on the attached credit report.

Since reinvestigation has not resolved my dispute, I want the following statement included in my credit report to set forth the nature of my dispute for others to see.

According to the Fair Credit Reporting Act, please send me a free updated copy of my credit report with the above statement included.

I assume that 30 days represents a "reasonable time" for completing this update, unless you immediately notify me.

Sincerely,

Name (Print)
Address, City, State, Zip
Social Security Number

Form 12

Date:

Address:

Re: Request For Addition of Supplementary Credit History Information

Dear Sir/Madam:

Please include in my credit report the supplemental information attached.

According to the Fair Credit Reporting Act (FCRA), 15 USC section 1681b, "It is the purpose of this title (FCRA) to require that consumer reporting agencies adopt reasonable procedures for meeting the needs of commerce for consumer credit, personnel, insurance, and other information in a manner which is fair and equitable to the consumer, with regard to the confidentiality, accuracy, relevancy, and proper utilization of such information in accordance with the requirements of this title." The intent of the FCRA includes recording supplementary credit information if requested by a consumer.

Accordingly, I hereby request that you add the attached history of payments, under the FCRA, 15 USC section 1681i.

Thank you for your attention. Please inform me within 30 days of your compliance with the 15 USC section 1681e requirements that a consumer's credit report should reflect "completeness and accuracy" within a "reasonable" time after notification by the consumer.

Sincerely,

Name (Print)
Address, City, State, Zip
Social Security Number

Fair Credit Reporting Act

s 1681. Congressional findings and statement of purpose

(a) The Congress makes the following findings:

(1) The banking system is dependent upon fair and accurate credit reporting.

Inaccurate credit reports directly impair the efficiency of the banking system, and unfair credit reporting methods undermine the public confidence which is essential to the continued functioning of the banking system.

(2) An elaborate mechanism has been developed for investigating and evaluating the credit worthiness, credit standing, credit capacity, character, and general reputation of consumers.

(3) Consumer reporting agencies have assumed a vital role in assembling and evaluating consumer credit and other information on consumers.

(4) There is a need to insure that consumer reporting agencies exercise their grave responsibilities with fairness, impartiality, and a respect for the consumer's right to privacy.

(b) It is the purpose of this subchapter to require that consumer reporting agencies adopt reasonable procedures for meeting the needs of commerce for consumer credit, personnel, insurance, and other information in a manner which is fair and equitable to the consumer, with regard to the confidentiality, accuracy, relevancy, and proper utilization of such information in accordance with the requirements of this subchapter.

s 1681a. Definitions; rules of construction

(a) Definitions and rules of construction set forth in this section are applicable for the purposes of this subchapter.

(b) The term "person" means any individual, partnership, corporation, trust, estate, cooperative, association, government or governmental subdivision or agency, or other entity.

(c) The term "consumer" means an individual.

(d) The term "consumer report" means any written, oral, or other communication of any information by a consumer reporting agency bearing on a consumer's credit worthiness, credit standing, credit capacity, character, general reputation, personal characteristics, or mode of living which is used or expected to be used or collected in whole or in part for the purpose of serving as a factor in establishing the consumer's eligibility for creditors insurance to be used primarily for

(1) personal, family, or household purposes, or

(2) employment purposes, or

(3) other purposes authorized under section 1681b of this title.

<u>The term does not include</u>

(A) any report containing information solely as to transactions or experiences between the consumer and the person making the report;

(B) any authorization or approval of a specific extension of credit directly or indirectly by the issuer of a credit card or similar device; or

(C) any report in which a person who has been requested by a third party to make a specific extension of credit directly or indirectly to a consumer conveys his decision with respect to such request, if the third party advises the consumer of the name and address of the person to whom the request was made and such person makes the disclosures to the consumer required under section 1681m of this title.

(D) The term "investigative consumer report" means a consumer report or portion thereof in which information on a consumer's character, general reputation, personal characteristics, or mode of living is obtained through personal interviews with neighbors, friends, or associates of the consumer reported on or with others with whom he is acquainted or who may have knowledge concerning any such items of information. However, such information shall not include specific factual information on a consumer's credit record obtained directly from a creditor of the consumer or from a consumer reporting agency when such information was obtained directly from a creditor of the consumer or from the consumer.

(E) The term "consumer reporting agency" means any person which, for monetary fees, dues, or on a cooperative nonprofit basis, regularly engages in whole or in part in the practice of assembling or evaluating consumer credit information or other information on consumers for the purpose of furnishing consumer reports to third parties, and which uses any means or facility of interstate commerce for the purpose of preparing or furnishing consumer reports.

(F) The term "file," when used in connection with information on any consumer, means all of the information on that consumer recorded and retained by a consumer reporting agency regardless of how the information is stored.

(G) The term "employment purposes" when used in connection with a consumer report means a report used for the purpose of evaluating a consumer for employment, promotion, reassignment or retention as an employee.

(H) The term "medical information" means information or records obtained, with the consent of the individual to whom it relates, from licensed physicians or medical practitioners, hospitals, clinics, or other medical or medically related facilities.

(I) Definitions relating to child support obligations

(1) The term "overdue support" has the meaning given to such term in section 666(e) of Title 42.

(2) The term "state or local child support enforcement agency" means a state or local agency which administers a state or local program for establishing and enforcing child support obligations.

s 1681b. Permissible purposes of consumer reports

A consumer reporting agency may furnish a consumer report under the following circumstances and no other:

(a) In response to the order of a court having jurisdiction to issue such an order, or a subpoena issued in connection with proceedings before a federal grand jury.

(b) In accordance with the written instructions of the consumer to whom it relates.

(c) To a person which it has reason to believe:

(1) intends to use the information in connection with a credit transaction involving the consumer on whom the information is to be furnished and involving the extension of credit to, or review or collection of an account of, the consumer; or

(2) intends to use the information for employment purposes; or

(3) intends to use the information in connection with the underwriting of insurance involving the consumer; or

(4) intends to use the information in connection with a determination of the consumer's eligibility for a license or other benefit granted by a governmental instrumentality required by law to consider an applicant's financial responsibility or status; or

(5) otherwise has a legitimate business need for the information in connection with a business transaction involving the consumer.

s 1681c. Reporting of obsolete information prohibited

(a) Except as authorized under subsection (b) of this section, no consumer reporting agency may make any consumer report containing any of the following items of information:

(1) Cases under Title 11 or under the Bankruptcy Act that, from the date of entry of the order for relief or the date of adjudication, as the case may be, antedate the report by more than 10 years.

(2) Suits and judgments which, from date of entry, antedate the report by more than seven years or until the governing statute of limitations has expired, whichever is the longer period.

(3) Paid tax liens which, from date of payment, antedate the report by more than seven years.

(4) Accounts placed for collection or charged to profit and loss which antedate the report by more than seven years.

(5) Records of arrest, indictment, or conviction of crime which, from date of disposition, release, or parole, antedate the report by more than seven years.

(6) Any other adverse item of information which antedates the report by more than seven years.

(b) The provisions of subsection (a) of this section are not applicable in the case of any consumer credit report to be used in connection with–

(1) a credit transaction involving, or which may reasonably be expected to involve, a principal amount of $50,000 or more;

(2) the underwriting of life insurance involving, or which may reasonably be expected to involve, a face amount of $50,000 or more; or

(3) the employment of any individual at an annual salary which equals, or which may reasonably be expected to equal, $20,000 or more.

s 1681d. Disclosure of investigative consumer reports

(a) Disclosure of fact of preparation

A person may not procure or cause to be prepared an investigative consumer report on any consumer unless:

(1) it is clearly and accurately disclosed to the consumer that an investigative consumer report including information as to his character, general reputation, personal characteristics, and mode of living, whichever are applicable, may be made, and such disclosure (A) is made in a writing mailed, or otherwise delivered, to the consumer, not later than three days after the date on which the report was first requested, and (B) includes a statement informing the consumer of his right to request the additional disclosures provided for under subsection (b) of this section; or

(2) the report is to be used for employment purposes for which the consumer has not specifically applied.

(b) Disclosure on request of nature and scope of investigation

Any person who procures or causes to be prepared an investigative consumer report on any consumer shall, upon written request made by the consumer within a reasonable period of time after the receipt by him of the disclosure required by subsection (a)(1) of this section, shall make a complete and accurate disclosure of the nature and scope of the investigation requested. This disclosure shall be made in a writing mailed, or otherwise delivered, to the consumer not later than five days after the date on which the request for such disclosure was received from the consumer or such report was first requested, whichever is the later.

(c) Limitation on liability upon showing of reasonable procedures for compliance with provisions

No person may be held liable for any violation of subsection (a) or (b) of this section if he shows by a preponderance of the evidence that at the time of the violation he maintained reasonable procedures to assure compliance with subsection (a) or (b) of this section.

s 1681e. Compliance procedures

(a) Every consumer reporting agency shall maintain reasonable procedures designed to avoid violations of section 1681c of this title and to limit the furnishing of consumer reports to the purposes listed under section 1681b of this title. These procedures shall require that prospective users of the information identify themselves, certify the purposes for which the information is sought, and certify that the information will be used for no other purpose. Every consumer reporting agency shall make a reasonable effort to verify the identity of a new prospective user and the uses certified by such prospective user prior to furnishing such user a consumer report. No consumer reporting agency may furnish a consumer report to any person if it has reasonable grounds for believing that the consumer report will not be used for a purpose listed in section 1681b of this title.

(b) Whenever a consumer reporting agency prepares a consumer report it shall follow reasonable procedures to assure maximum possible accuracy of the information concerning the individual about whom the report relates.

s 1681f. Disclosures to governmental agencies

Notwithstanding the provisions of section 1681b of this title, a consumer reporting agency may furnish identifying information respecting any consumer, limited to his name, address, former addresses, places of employment, or former places of employment, to a governmental agency.

s 1681g. Disclosures to consumers

(a) Every consumer reporting agency shall, upon request and proper identification of any consumer, clearly and accurately disclose to the consumer:

(1) The nature and substance of all information (except medical information) in its files on the consumer at the time of the request.

(2) The sources of the information; except that the sources of information acquired solely for use in preparing an investigative consumer report and actually used for no

other purpose need not be disclosed. Provided that in the event an action is brought under this subchapter, such sources shall be available to the plaintiff under appropriate discovery procedures in the court in which the action is brought.

(3) The recipients of any consumer report on the consumer which it has furnished:

(a) for employment purposes within the two-year period preceding the request, and

(b) for any other purpose within the six-month period preceding the request.

(c) The requirements of subsection (a) of this section respecting the disclosure of sources of information and the recipients of consumer reports do not apply to information received or consumer reports furnished prior to the effective date of this subchapter except to the extent that the matter involved is contained in the files of the consumer reporting agency on that date.

s 1681h. Conditions of disclosure to consumers

(a) Times and notice

A consumer reporting agency shall make the disclosures required under section 1681g of this title during normal business hours and on reasonable notice.

(b) Identification of consumer

The disclosures required under section 1681g of this title shall be made to the consumer:

(1) in person if he appears in person and furnishes proper identification; or

(2) by telephone if he has made a written request, with proper identification, for telephone disclosure and the toll charge, if any, for the telephone call is prepaid by or charged directly to the consumer.

(c) Trained personnel

Any consumer reporting agency shall provide trained personnel to explain to the consumer any information furnished to him pursuant to section 1681g of this title.

(d) Persons accompanying consumer

The consumer shall be permitted to be accompanied by one other person of his choosing, who shall furnish reasonable identification. A consumer reporting agency may require the consumer to furnish a written statement granting permission to the consumer reporting agency to discuss the consumer's file in such person's presence.

(e) Limitation of liability

Except as provided in sections 1681n and 1681o of this title, no consumer may bring any action or proceeding in the nature of defamation, invasion of privacy, or negligence with respect to the reporting of information against any consumer reporting agency, any user of information, or any person who furnishes information to a consumer reporting agency, based on information disclosed pursuant to section 1681g, 1681h, or 1681m of this title, except as to false information furnished with malice or willful intent to injure such consumer.

s 1681i. Procedure in case of disputed accuracy

(a) Dispute; reinvestigation

If the completeness or accuracy of any item of information contained in his file is disputed by a consumer, and such dispute is directly conveyed to the consumer reporting agency by the consumer, the consumer reporting agency shall within a reasonable period of time reinvestigate and record the current status of that information unless it has reasonable grounds to believe that the dispute by the consumer is frivolous or irrelevant. If after such reinvestigation such information is found to be inaccurate or can no longer be verified, the consumer reporting agency shall promptly delete such information. The presence of contradictory information in the consumer's file does not in and of itself constitute reasonable grounds for believing the dispute is frivolous or irrelevant.

(b) Statement of dispute

If the reinvestigation does not resolve the dispute, the consumer may file a brief statement setting forth the nature of the dispute. The consumer reporting agency may limit such statements to not more than one hundred words if it provides the consumer with assistance in writing a clear summary of the dispute.

(c) Notification of consumer dispute in subsequent consumer reports

Whenever a statement of a dispute is filed, unless there is reasonable grounds to believe that it is frivolous or irrelevant, the consumer reporting agency shall, in any subsequent consumer report containing the information in question, clearly note that it is disputed by the consumer and provide either the consumer's statement or a clear and accurate codification or summary thereof.

(d) Notification of deletion of disputed information

Following any deletion of information which is found to be inaccurate or whose accuracy can no longer be verified or any notation as to disputed information, the consumer reporting agency shall, at the request of the consumer, furnish notification that the item has been deleted or the statement, codification or summary pursuant to subsection (b) or (c) of this section to any person specifically designated by the consumer who has within two years prior thereto received a consumer report for employment purposes, or within six months prior thereto received a consumer report for any other purpose, which contained the deleted or disputed information. The consumer reporting agency shall clearly and conspicuously disclose to the consumer his rights to make such a request. Such disclosure shall be made at or prior to the time the information is deleted or the consumer's statement regarding the disputed information is received.

s 1681j. Charges for disclosures

A consumer reporting agency shall make all disclosures pursuant to section 1681g of this title and furnish all consumer reports pursuant to section 1681i(d) of this title without charge to the consumer if, within thirty days after receipt by such consumer of a notification pursuant to section 1681m of this title or notification from a debt collection agency affiliated with such consumer reporting agency stating that the consumer's credit rating may be or has been adversely affected, the consumer makes a request under section 1681g or 1681i(d) of this title. Otherwise, the consumer reporting agency may impose a reasonable charge on the consumer for making disclosure to such consumer pursuant to section 1681g of this title, the charge for which shall be indicated to the consumer prior to making disclosure; and for furnishing notifications, statements, summaries, or codifications to a person designated by the consumer pursuant to section 1681i(d) of this title, the charge for which shall be indicated to the consumer prior to furnishing such information and shall not exceed the charge that the consumer reporting agency would impose on each designated recipient for a consumer report except that no charge may be made for notifying such persons of the deletion of information which is found to be inaccurate or which can no longer be verified.

s 1681k. Public record information for employment purposes

A consumer reporting agency which furnishes a consumer report for employment purposes and which for that purpose compiles and reports items of information on consumers which are matters of public record and are likely to have an adverse effect upon a consumer's ability to obtain employment shall:

(1) at the time such public record information is reported to the user of such consumer report, notify the consumer of the fact that public record information is being reported by the consumer reporting agency, together with the name and address of the person to whom such information is being reported; or

(2) maintain strict procedures designed to insure that whenever public record information which is likely to have an adverse effect on a consumer's ability to obtain employment is reported it is complete and up to date. For purposes of this paragraph, items of public record relating to arrests, indictments, convictions, suits, tax liens, and outstanding judgments shall be considered up to date if the current public record status of the item at the time of the report is reported.

s 1681l. Restrictions on investigative consumer reports

Whenever a consumer reporting agency prepares an investigative consumer report, no adverse information in the consumer report (other than information which is a matter of public record) may be included in a subsequent consumer report unless such adverse information has been verified in the process of making such subsequent consumer report, or the adverse information was received within the three-month period preceding the date the subsequent report is furnished.

s 1681m. Requirements on users of consumer reports

(a) Adverse action based on reports of consumer reporting agencies

Whenever credit or insurance for personal, family, or household purposes, or employment involving a consumer is denied or the charge for such credit or insurance is increased either wholly or partly because of information contained in a consumer report from a consumer reporting agency, the user of the consumer report shall so advise the consumer against whom such adverse action has been taken and supply the name and address of the consumer reporting agency making the report.

(b) Adverse action based on reports of persons other than consumer reporting agencies

Whenever credit for personal, family, or household purposes involving a consumer is denied or the charge for such credit is increased either wholly or partly because of information obtained from a person other than a consumer reporting agency bearing upon the consumer's creditworthiness, credit standing, credit capacity, character, general reputation, personal characteristics, or mode of living, the user of such information shall, within a reasonable period of time, upon the consumer's written request for the reasons for such adverse action received within sixty days after learning of such adverse action, disclose the nature of the information to the consumer. The user of such information shall clearly and accurately disclose to the consumer his right to make such written request at the time such adverse action is communicated to the consumer.

(c) Reasonable procedures to assure compliance

No person shall be held liable for any violation of this section if he shows by a preponderance of the evidence that at the time of the alleged violation he maintained reasonable procedures to assure compliance with the provisions of subsections (a) and (b) of this section.

s 1681n. Civil liability for willful noncompliance

Any consumer reporting agency or user of information which willfully fails to comply with any requirement imposed under this subchapter with respect to any consumer is liable to that consumer in an amount equal to the sum of:

(1) any actual damages sustained by the consumer as a result of the failure;

(2) such amount of punitive damages as the court may allow; and

(3) in the case of any successful action to enforce any liability under this section, the costs of the action together with reasonable attorney's fees as determined by the court.

s 1681o. Civil liability for negligent noncompliance

Any consumer reporting agency or user of information which is negligent in failing to comply with any requirement imposed under this subchapter with respect to any consumer is liable to that consumer in an amount equal to the sum of:

(1) any actual damages sustained by the consumer as a result of the failure;

(2) in the case of any successful action to enforce any liability under this section, the costs of the action together with reasonable attorney's fees as determined by the court.

s 1681p. Jurisdiction of courts; limitation of actions

An action to enforce any liability created under this subchapter may be brought in any appropriate United States district court without regard to the amount in controversy, or in any other court of competent jurisdiction, within two years from the date on which the liability arises, except that where a defendant has materially and willfully misrepresented any information required under this subchapter to be disclosed to an individual and the information so misrepresented is material to the establishment of the defendant's liability to that individual under this subchapter, the action may be brought at any time within two years after discovery by the individual of the misrepresentation.

s 1681q. Obtaining information under false pretenses

Any person who knowingly and willfully obtains information on a consumer from a consumer reporting agency under false pretenses shall be fined not more than $5,000 or imprisoned not more than one year, or both.

s 1681r. Unauthorized disclosures by officers or employees

Any officer or employee of a consumer reporting agency who knowingly and willfully provides information concerning an individual from the agency's files to a person not authorized to receive that information shall be fined not more than $5,000 or imprisoned not more than one year, or both.

s 1681s. Administrative enforcement

(a) Federal Trade Commission; powers

Compliance with the requirements imposed under this subchapter shall be enforced under the Federal Trade Commission Act by the Federal Trade Commission with respect to consumer reporting agencies and all other persons subject thereto, except to the extent that enforcement of the requirements imposed under this subchapter is specifically committed to some other government agency under subsection (b) hereof. For the purpose of the exercise by the Federal Trade Commission of its functions and powers under the Federal Trade Commission Act, a violation of any requirement or prohibition imposed under this subchapter shall constitute an unfair or deceptive act or practice in commerce in violation of section 5(a) of the Federal Trade Commission Act and shall be subject to enforcement by the Federal Trade Commission under section 5(b) thereof with respect to any consumer reporting agency or person subject to enforcement by the Federal Trade Commission pursuant to this subsection, irrespective of whether that person is engaged in commerce or meets any other jurisdictional tests in the Federal Trade Commission Act. The Federal Trade Commission shall have such procedural, investigative, and enforcement powers, including the power to issue procedural rules in enforcing compliance with the requirements imposed under this subchapter and to require the filing of reports, the production of documents, and the appearance of witnesses as though the applicable terms and conditions of the Federal Trade Commission Act were part of this subchapter. Any person violating any of the provisions of this subchapter shall be subject to the penalties and entitled to the privileges and immunities provided in the Federal Trade Commission Act as though the applicable terms and provisions thereof were part of this subchapter.

(b) Other administrative bodies

Compliance with the requirements imposed under this subchapter with respect to consumer reporting agencies and persons who use consumer reports from such agencies shall be enforced under–

(1) section 8 of the Federal Deposit Insurance Act [12 U.S.C.A. s 1818], in the case of–

(a) national banks, and Federal branches and Federal agencies of foreign banks, by the Office of the Comptroller of the Currency;

(b) member banks of the Federal Reserve System (other than national banks), branches and agencies of foreign banks (other than Federal branches, Federal agencies, and insured State branches of foreign banks), commercial lending companies owned or controlled by foreign banks, and organizations operating under section 25 or 25(a) of the Federal Reserve Act [12 U.S.C.A. ss 601 et seq., 611 et seq.], by the Board of Governors of the Federal Reserve System; and

(c) banks insured by the Federal Deposit Insurance Corporation (other than members of the Federal Reserve System) and insured State branches of foreign banks, by the Board of Directors of the Federal Deposit Insurance Corporation;

(2) Section 8 of the Federal Deposit Insurance Act [12 U.S.C.A. s 1818], by the Director of the Office of Thrift Supervision, in the case of a savings association the deposits of which are insured by the Federal Deposit Insurance Corporation.

(3) the Federal Credit Union Act, by the Administrator of the National Credit Union Administration with respect to any Federal credit union;

(4) subtitle IV of Title 49, by the Interstate Commerce Commission with respect to any common carrier subject to such subtitle;

(5) the Federal Aviation Act of 1958, by the Secretary of Transportation with respect to any air carrier or foreign air carrier subject to that Act; and

(6) the Packers and Stockyards Act, 1921 (except as provided in section 406 of that Act), by the Secretary of Agriculture with respect to any activities subject to that Act.

The terms used in paragraph (1) that are not defined in this subchapter or otherwise defined in section 3(s) of the Federal Deposit Insurance Act (12 U.S.C. 1813(s)) shall have the meaning given to them in section 1(b) of the International Banking Act of 1978 (12 U.S.C. 3101).

(c) Enforcement under other authority

For the purpose of the exercise by any agency referred to in subsection (b) of this section of its powers under any Act referred to in that subsection, a violation of any requirement imposed under this subchapter shall be deemed to be a violation of a requirement imposed under that Act. In addition to its powers under any provision of law specifically referred to in subsection (b) of this section, each of the agencies referred to in that subsection may exercise, for the purpose of enforcing compliance with any requirement imposed under this subchapter any other authority conferred on it by law.

s 1681s-1. Information on overdue child support obligations

Notwithstanding any other provision of this subchapter, a consumer reporting agency shall include in any consumer report furnished by the agency in accordance with section 1681b of this title, any information on the failure of the consumer to pay overdue support which:

(1) is provided:

(a) to the consumer reporting agency by a State or local child support enforcement agency; or

(b) to the consumer reporting agency and verified by any local, State, or Federal Government agency; and

(2) antedates the report by 7 years or less.

s 1681t. Relation to State laws

This subchapter does not annul, alter, affect, or exempt any person subject to the provisions of this subchapter from complying with the laws of any State with respect to the collection, distribution, or use of any information on consumers, except to the extent that those laws are inconsistent with any provision of this subchapter, and then only to the extent of the inconsistency.

Glossary of useful terms

A-C

Agent banks - smaller banks that act as credit card agents for larger banks.

Annual membership fee - a charge paid by holders of some credit cards for the privilege of using that card.

Annual percentage rate (APR) - the percentage of the loan that is paid to the creditor, as established by each state.

ATM cards - plastic cards issued by banks for use in automated teller machines.

ATM machines - automated teller machines.

Bank card system - since most banks cannot afford to support all of the functions associated with credit cards, smaller banks contract with larger banks for card-related services.

Bankruptcy - the legal process under which the debtor is given a new start and the creditors receive a fair distribution of the debtor's assets.

Chain - the line of support that extend from the major bank through its agent banks.

Charge off - to charge an account off to profit and loss because the debt is considered uncollectible.

Collateral - something of value that can be sold by the lender in the event of a default on the loan.

Collection agency - a company that attempts to collect bad debts for a percentage of what is collected.

Consumer Statement - a written statement by the consumer disputing the accuracy of certain information in the credit report.

Co-signer - a person who has good credit and agrees to assume responsibility for your debts in the event that you default.

Credit history - a record indicating your trustworthiness and ability to repay a loan.

C-R

Credit report - a report issued by a credit reporting agency listing five types of information: 1) Identifying information 2) Account information 3) Public record information 4) Credit report requests and 5) A consumer statement

Credit reporting agency - a company or bureau that receives and reports information on consumers' credit reports.

Credit scoring system - a system used to rate creditworthiness.

Creditor - one who extends credit: bank, store, credit card company, etc.

Debit card - a card that allows money to be electronically deducted from an account to pay a bill or make a purchase.

Ding - a negative or neutral entry or remark on a credit report.

Finance charge - see annual percentage rate (APR).

Fair Credit Reporting Act - a federal law that protects against credit abuses.

Federal Trade Commission - the federal agency responsible for bringing legal action against a credit bureau.

Foreclosure - repossession and sale of property that has been used as collateral for a debt that has not been paid.

Grace period - the period during which no interest is charged for credit card usage.

Historical status - a record of your monthly payments.

LIBOR - London Interbank Offered Rate.

Major bank - the largest bank in a chain, which provides credit card services to its agent banks.

PIN - Personal identification number issued with each ATM card.

Reasonable time - federal law requires the credit bureau to respond to a consumer dispute within a reasonable period of time (usually no longer than eight weeks) or the agency is in default.

Repayment history - creditors report your credit payments as either delinquent (negative), regular (positive), or neutral (non-rated).

S-W

Secured credit card - a credit card backed by the holder's cash deposit in a designated savings account.

Short-term-debt-to-income ratio - the percentage of your annual income your short term debt represents.

Subscribers - businesses that pay a credit reporting agency for access to the files of people who bought on credit.

Transaction fee - a fee charged by some credit cards for each use of the card.

20 percent rule - a guideline that suggests that short-term debt be no more than 20 percent of your annual income.

Win-win offer - trading money for a positive credit rating on your credit report.

How To Save On Attorney Fees

Millions of Americans know they need legal protection, whether it's to get agreements in writing, protect themselves from lawsuits, or document business transactions. But too often these basic but important legal matters are neglected because of something else millions of Americans know: legal services are expensive.

They don't have to be. In response to the demand for affordable legal protection and services, there are now specialized clinics that process simple documents. Paralegals help people prepare legal claims on a freelance basis. People find they can handle their own legal affairs with do-it-yourself legal guides and kits. Indeed, this book is a part of this growing trend.

Highlight

When are these alternatives to a lawyer appropriate? If you hire an attorney, how can you make sure you're getting good advice for a reasonable fee? Most importantly, do you know how to lower your legal expenses?

When are these alternatives to a lawyer appropriate? If you hire an attorney, how can you make sure you're getting good advice for a reasonable fee? Most importantly, do you know how to lower your legal expenses?

When there is no alternative

Make no mistake: serious legal matters require a lawyer. The tips in this book can help you reduce your legal fees, but there is no alternative to good professional legal services in certain circumstances:

- When you are charged with a felony, you are a repeat offender, or jail is possible.
- When a substantial amount of money or property is at stake in a lawsuit.
- When you are a party in an adversarial divorce or custody case.
- When you are an alien facing deportation.

- When you are the plaintiff in a personal injury suit that involves large sums of money.
- When you're involved in very important transactions.

Are you sure you want to take it to court?

Consider the following questions before you pursue legal action:

 ***What are your financial resources?***

Money buys experienced attorneys, and experience wins over first-year lawyers and public defenders. Even with a strong case, you may save money by not going to court. Yes, people win millions in court. But for every big winner there are ten plaintiffs who either lose or win so little that litigation wasn't worth their effort.

Highlight

Even with a strong case, you may save money by not going to court.

 ***Do you have the time and energy for a trial?***

Courts are overbooked, and by the time your case is heard your initial zeal may have grown cold. If you can, make a reasonable settlement out of court. On personal matters, like a divorce or custody case, consider the emotional toll on all parties. Any legal case will affect you in some way. You will need time away from work. A newsworthy case may bring press coverage. Your loved ones, too, may face publicity. There is usually good reason to settle most cases quickly, quietly, and economically.

How can you settle your disputes without litigation?

Consider *mediation.* In mediation, each party pays half the mediator's fee and, together, they attempt to work out a compromise informally. *Binding arbitration* is another alternative. For a small fee, a trained specialist serves as judge, hears both sides, and hands down a ruling that both parties have agreed to accept.

So you need an attorney

Having done your best to avoid litigation, if you still find yourself headed for court, you will need an attorney. To get the right attorney at a reasonable cost, be guided by these four questions:

 ***What type of case is it?***

You don't seek a foot doctor for a toothache. Find an attorney experienced in your type of legal problem. If you can get recommendations from clients who have recently won similar cases, do so.

Where will the trial be held?

You want a lawyer familiar with that court system and one who knows the court personnel and the local protocol – which can vary from one locality to another.

 ***Should you hire a large or small firm?***

Hiring a senior partner at a large and prestigious law firm sounds reassuring, but chances are the actual work will be handled by associates – at high rates. Small firms may give your case more attention but, with fewer resources, take longer to get the work done.

Highlight

High fees may reflect a firm's luxurious offices, high-paid staff and unmonitored expenses, while low estimates may mean "unexpected" costs later.

 ***What can you afford?***

Hire an attorney you can afford, of course, but know what a fee quote includes. High fees may reflect a firm's luxurious offices, high-paid staff and unmonitored expenses, while low estimates may mean "unexpected" costs later. Ask for a written estimate of all costs and anticipated expenses.

How to find a good lawyer

Whether you need an attorney quickly or you're simply open to future possibilities, here are seven nontraditional methods for finding your lawyer:

1. ***Word of mouth:*** Successful lawyers develop reputations. Your friends, business associates and other professionals are potential referral sources. But beware of hiring a friend. Keep the client-attorney relationship strictly business.
2. ***Directories:*** The Yellow Pages and the Martin-Hubbell Lawyer Directory (in your local library) can help you locate a lawyer with the right education, background and expertise for your case.
3. ***Databases:*** A paralegal should be able to run a quick computer search of local attorneys for you using the Westlaw or Lexis database.
4. ***State bar association:*** Bar associations are listed in phone books. Along with lawyer referrals, your bar association can direct you to low-cost legal clinics or specialists in your area.
5. ***Law schools:*** Did you know that a legal clinic run by a law school gives law students hands-on experience? This may fit your legal needs. A third-year law student loaded with enthusiasm and a little experience might fill the bill quite inexpensively—or even for free.
6. ***Advertisements:*** Ads are a lawyer's business card. If a "TV attorney" seems to have a good track record with your kind of case, why not call? Just don't be swayed by the glamour of a high-

profile attorney.

7. ***Your own ad:*** A small ad describing the qualifications and legal expertise you're seeking, placed in a local bar association journal, may get you just the lead you need.

How to hire and work with your attorney

No matter how you hear about an attorney, you must interview him or her in person. Call the office during business hours and ask to speak to the attorney directly. Then explain your case briefly and mention how you obtained the attorney's name. If the attorney sounds interested and knowledgeable, arrange for a visit.

Highlight

Explain your case briefly and mention how you obtained the attorney's name. If the attorney sounds interested and knowledgeable, arrange for a visit.

The ten-point visit:

1. Note the address. This is a good indication of the rates to expect.
2. Note the condition of the offices. File-laden desks and poorly maintained work space may indicate a poorly run firm.
3. Look for up-to-date computer equipment and an adequate complement of support personnel.
4. Note the appearance of the attorney. How will he or she impress a judge or jury?
5. Is the attorney attentive? Does the attorney take notes, ask questions, follow up on points you've mentioned?
6. Ask what schools he or she has graduated from, and feel free to check credentials with the state bar association.
7. Does the attorney have a good track record with your type of case?
8. Does he or she explain legal terms to you in plain English?
9. Are the firm's costs reasonable?
10. Will the attorney provide references?

Hiring the attorney

Having chosen your attorney, make sure all the terms are agreeable. Send letters to any other attorneys you have interviewed, thanking them for their time and interest in your case and explaining that you have retained another attorney's services.

Request a letter from your new attorney outlining your retainer agreement. The letter should list all fees you will be responsible for as well as the billing arrangement. Did you arrange to pay in installments? This should be noted in your retainer agreement.

Controlling legal costs

Legal fees and expenses can get out of control easily, but the client who is willing to put in the effort can keep legal costs manageable. Work out a budget with your attorney. Create a timeline for your case. Estimate the costs involved in each step.

Highlight

Don't be afraid to question legal bills. It's your case and your money!

Legal fees can be straightforward. Some lawyers charge a fixed rate for a specific project. Others charge contingency fees (they collect a percentage of your recovery, usually 35-50 percent, if you win and nothing if you lose). But most attorneys prefer to bill by the hour. Expenses can run the gamut, with one hourly charge for taking depositions and another for making copies.

Have your attorney give you a list of charges for services rendered and an itemized monthly bill. The bill should explain the service performed, who performed the work, when the service was provided, how long it took, and how the service benefits your case.

Ample opportunity abounds in legal billing for dishonesty and greed. There is also plenty of opportunity for knowledgeable clients to cut their bills significantly if they know what to look for. Asking the right questions and setting limits on fees is smart and can save you a bundle. Don't be afraid to question legal bills. It's your case and your money!

When the bill arrives

- ***Retainer fees:*** You should already have a written retainer agreement. Ideally, the retainer fee applies toward case costs, and your agreement puts that in writing. Protect yourself by escrowing the retainer fee until the case has been handled to your satisfaction.
- ***Office visit charges:*** Track your case and all documents, correspondence, and bills. Diary all dates, deadlines and questions you want to ask your attorney during your next office visit. This keeps expensive office visits focused and productive, with more accomplished in less time. If your attorney charges less for phone consultations than office visits, reserve visits for those tasks that must be done in person.

- ***Phone bills:*** This is where itemized bills are essential. Who made the call, who was spoken to, what was discussed, when was the call made, and how long did it last? Question any charges that seem unnecessary or excessive (over 60 minutes).
- ***Administrative costs:*** Your case may involve hundreds, if not thousands, of documents: motions, affidavits, depositions, interrogatories, bills, memoranda, and letters. Are they all necessary? Understand your attorney's case strategy before paying for an endless stream of costly documents.
- ***Associate and paralegal fees:*** Note in your retainer agreement which staff people will have access to your file. Then you'll have an informed and efficient staff working on your case, and you'll recognize their names on your bill. Of course, your attorney should handle the important part of your case, but less costly paralegals or associates may handle routine matters more economically. Note: Some firms expect their associates to meet a quota of billable hours, although the time spent is not always warranted. Review your bill. Does the time spent make sense for the document in question? Are several staff involved in matters that should be handled by one person? Don't be afraid to ask questions. And withhold payment until you have satisfactory answers.

Highlight

Note in your retainer agreement which staff people will have access to your file. Then you'll have an informed and efficient staff working on your case, and you'll recognize their names on your bill.

- ***Court stenographer fees:*** Depositions and court hearings require costly transcripts and stenographers. This means added expenses. Keep an eye on these costs.
- ***Copying charges:*** Your retainer fee should limit the number of copies made of your complete file. This is in your legal interest, because multiple files mean multiple chances others may access your confidential information. It is also in your financial interest, because copying costs can be astronomical.
- ***Fax costs:*** As with the phone and copier, the fax can easily run up costs. Set a limit.
- ***Postage charges:*** Be aware of how much it costs to send a legal document overnight, or a registered letter. Offer to pick up or deliver expensive items when it makes sense.
- ***Filing fees:*** Make it clear to your attorney that you want to minimize the number of court filings in your case. Watch your bill and question any filing that seems unnecessary.
- ***Document production fee:*** Turning over documents to your

Highlight

Surprise costs are so routine they're predictable. Budget a few thousand dollars over what you estimate your case will cost. It usually is needed.

opponent is mandatory and expensive. If you're faced with reproducing boxes of documents, consider having the job done by a commercial firm rather than your attorney's office.

- ***Research and investigations:*** Pay only for photographs that can be used in court. Can you hire a photographer at a lower rate than what your attorney charges? Reserve that right in your retainer agreement. Database research can also be extensive and expensive; if your attorney uses Westlaw or Nexis, set limits on the research you will pay for.
- ***Expert witnesses:*** Question your attorney if you are expected to pay for more than a reasonable number of expert witnesses. Limit the number to what is essential to your case.
- ***Technology costs:*** Avoid videos, tape recordings, and graphics if you can use old-fashioned diagrams to illustrate your case.
- ***Travel expenses:*** Travel expenses for those connected to your case can be quite costly unless you set a maximum budget. Check all travel-related items on your bill, and make sure they are appropriate. Always question why the travel is necessary before you agree to pay for it.
- ***Appeals costs:*** Losing a case often means an appeal, but weigh the costs involved before you make that decision. If money is at stake, do a cost-benefit analysis to see if an appeal is financially justified.
- ***Monetary damages:*** Your attorney should be able to help you estimate the total damages you will have to pay if you lose a civil case. Always consider settling out of court rather than proceeding to trial when the trial costs will be high.
- ***Surprise costs:*** Surprise costs are so routine they're predictable. The judge may impose unexpected court orders on one or both sides, or the opposition will file an unexpected motion that increases your legal costs. Budget a few thousand dollars over what you estimate your case will cost. It usually is needed.
- ***Padded expenses:*** Assume your costs and expenses are legitimate. But some firms do inflate expenses—office supplies, database searches, copying, postage, phone bills—to bolster their bottom line. Request copies of bills your law firm receives from support services. If you are not the only client represented on a bill, determine those charges related to your case.

Keeping it legal without a lawyer

The best way to save legal costs is to avoid legal problems. There are hundreds of ways to decrease your chances of lawsuits and other nasty legal encounters. Most simply involve a little common sense. You can also use your own initiative to find and use the variety of self-help legal aid available to consumers.

11 situations in which you may not need a lawyer

Highlight

The best way to save legal costs is to avoid legal problems.

1. ***No-fault divorce:*** Married couples with no children, minimal property, and no demands for alimony can take advantage of divorce mediation services. A lawyer should review your divorce agreement before you sign it, but you will have saved a fortune in attorney fees. A marital or family counselor may save a seemingly doomed marriage, or help both parties move beyond anger to a calm settlement. Either way, counseling can save you money.
2. ***Wills:*** Do-it-yourself wills and living trusts are ideal for people with estates of less than $600,000. Even if an attorney reviews your final documents, a will kit allows you to read the documents, ponder your bequests, fill out sample forms, and discuss your wishes with your family at your leisure, without a lawyer's meter running.
3. ***Incorporating:*** Incorporating a small business can be done by any business owner. Your state government office provides the forms and instructions necessary. A visit to your state offices will probably be necessary to perform a business name check. A fee of $100-$200 is usually charged for processing your Articles of Incorporation. The rest is paperwork: filling out forms correctly; holding regular, official meetings; and maintaining accurate records.
4. ***Routine business transactions:*** Copyrights, for example, can be applied for by asking the US Copyright Office for the appropriate forms and brochures. The same is true of the US Patent and Trademark Office. If your business does a great deal of document preparation and research, hire a certified paralegal rather than paying an attorney's rates. Consider mediation or binding arbitration rather than going to court for a business dispute. Hire a human resources/benefits administrator to head off disputes

concerning discrimination or other employee charges.

5. ***Repairing bad credit:*** When money matters get out of hand, attorneys and bankruptcy should not be your first solution. Contact a credit counseling organization that will help you work out manageable payment plans so that everyone wins. It can also help you learn to manage your money better. A good company to start with is the Consumer Credit Counseling Service, 1-800-388-2227.

Highlight

If your business does a great deal of document preparation and research, hire a certified paralegal rather than paying an attorney's rates.

6. ***Small Claims Court:*** For legal grievances amounting to a few thousand dollars in damages, represent yourself in Small Claims Court. There is a small filing fee, forms to fill out, and several court visits necessary. If you can collect evidence, state your case in a clear and logical presentation, and come across as neat, respectful and sincere, you can succeed in Small Claims Court.
7. ***Traffic Court:*** Like Small Claims Court, Traffic Court may show more compassion to a defendant appearing without an attorney. If you are ticketed for a minor offense and want to take it to court, you will be asked to plead guilty or not guilty. If you plead guilty, you can ask for leniency in sentencing by presenting mitigating circumstances. Bring any witnesses who can support your story, and remember that presentation (some would call it acting ability) is as important as fact.
8. ***Residential zoning petition:*** If a homeowner wants to open a home business, build an addition, or make other changes that may affect his or her neighborhood, town approval is required. But you don't need a lawyer to fill out a zoning variance application, turn it in, and present your story at a public hearing. Getting local support before the hearing is the best way to assure a positive vote; contact as many neighbors as possible to reassure them that your plans won't adversely affect them or the neighborhood.
9. ***Government benefit applications:*** Applying for veterans' or unemployment benefits may be daunting, but the process doesn't require legal help. Apply for either immediately upon becoming eligible. Note: If your former employer contests your application for unemployment benefits and you have to defend yourself at a hearing, you may want to consider hiring an attorney.
10. ***Receiving government files:*** The Freedom of Information Act gives every American the right to receive copies of government information

about him or her. Write a letter to the appropriate state or federal agency, noting the precise information you want. List each document in a separate paragraph. Mention the Freedom of Information Act, and state that you will pay any expenses. Close with your signature and the address the documents should be sent to. An approved request may take six months to arrive. If it is refused on the grounds that the information is classified or violates another's privacy, send a letter of appeal explaining why the released information would not endanger anyone. Enlist the support of your local state or federal representative, if possible, to smooth the approval process.

11. ***Citizenship:*** Arriving in the United States to work and become a citizen is a process tangled in bureaucratic red tape, but it requires more perseverance than legal assistance. Immigrants can learn how to obtain a "Green Card," under what circumstances they can work, and what the requirements of citizenship are by contacting the Immigration Services or reading a good self-help book.

Highlight

Arriving in the United States to work and become a citizen is a process tangled in bureaucratic red tape, but it requires more perseverance than legal assistance.

Save more; it's E-Z

When it comes to saving attorneys' fees, E-Z Legal Forms is the consumer's best friend. America's largest publisher of self-help legal products offers legally valid forms for virtually every situation. E-Z Legal Kits and E-Z Legal Guides include all necessary forms with a simple-to-follow manual of instructions or a layman's book. E-Z Legal Books are a legal library of forms and documents for everyday business and personal needs. E-Z Legal Software provides those same forms on disk for customized documents at the touch of the keyboard.

You can add to your legal savvy and your ability to protect yourself, your loved ones, your business and your property with a range of self-help legal titles available through E-Z Legal Forms. See the product descriptions and order form at the back of this guide.

(*How To Save On Attorney Fees* was compiled and written by Valerie Hope Goldstein.)

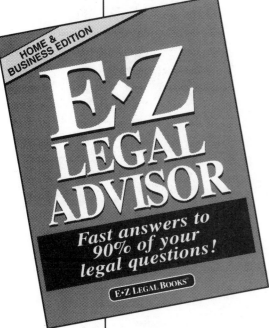

E•Z Legal Guides

- *Complete information*
- *Full instructions*
- *Do-it-yourself forms*
- *Only $14.95 each*

Living Will & Powers of Attorney

Dying with dignity is on the minds of every baby boomer and every boomer's parents. They are looking for information, for answers, for the forms they need to fill out now, while they are healthy. They'll find it all in one simple book, the *Guide to Living Will & Powers of Attorney*.

Stock No.: G106
$14.95 8.5" x 11"
128 pages Soft cover
ISBN 1-56382-406-X

Immigration

This simple guide explains the various ways America allows aliens to qualify for "green cards," offers step-by-step directions in the petition and application processes, and prepares immigrants to become naturalized citizens. An excellent reference book complete with federally required forms.

Stock No.: G113
$14.95 8.5" x 11"
176 pages Soft cover
ISBN 1-56382-413-2

Divorce

Spouses facing an amicable divorce shouldn't have to face off with contentious lawyers. This guide explains when a do-it-yourself divorce is appropriate, provides the forms necessary, takes the reader through the legal steps, and provides state-by-state information for filing for divorce.

Stock No.: G102
$14.95 8.5" x 11"
160 pages Soft cover
ISBN 1-56382-402-7

Credit Repair

Anyone can improve bad credit with the help of this guide. From discovering exactly what a credit report contains to challenging false information and turning unfavorable reports into glowing reports, it's all in this guide. Sample letters help the reader contact the right authorities and assert his or her consumer rights.

Stock No.: G103
$14.95 8.5" x 11"
176 pages Soft cover
ISBN 1-56382-403-5

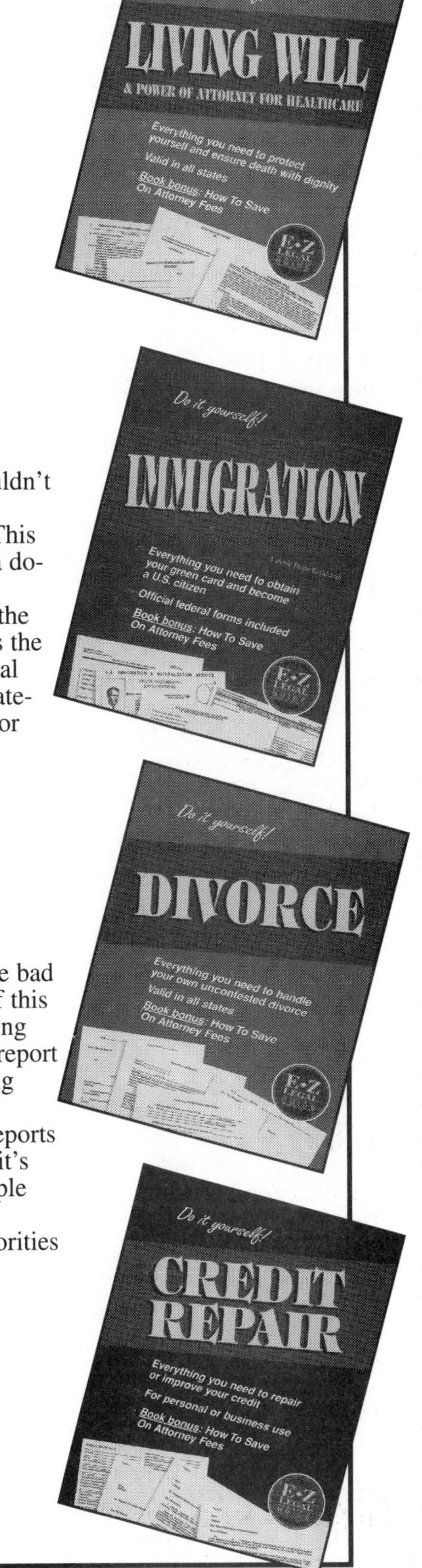

Bankruptcy

How does someone file bankruptcy without adding to their debts? With the *E-Z Legal Guide to Bankruptcy.* Takes the confusion out of bankruptcy by taking the reader through the forms, the law, even the state and federal exemptions.

Stock No.: G100
$14.95 8.5" x 11"
128 pages Soft cover
ISBN 1-56382-400-0

Small Claims Court

The reader prepares for his day in court with this guide, which explains the process for the plaintiff and the defendant, offers options to an actual court case, and more. For anyone who has ever thought about taking someone to court.

Stock No.: G109
$14.95 8.5" x 11"
128 pages Soft cover
ISBN 1-56382-409-4

Employment Law

This is a handy reference for anyone with questions about hiring, wages and benefits, privacy, discrimination, injuries, sexual harassment, unions, and unemployment. Written in simple language from the perspectives of both the employer and the employee.

Stock No.: G112
$14.95 8.5" x 11"
112 pages Soft cover
ISBN 1-56382-412-4

Traffic Court

For most American drivers, traffic tickets are an annoying fact of life. But sometimes the motorist doesn't deserve the ticket. This guide tells how and why to fight a ticket, and how to handle a police stop, read a traffic ticket, and take it to court and win.

Stock No.: G110
$14.95 8.5" x 11"
112 pages Soft cover
ISBN 1-56382-410-8

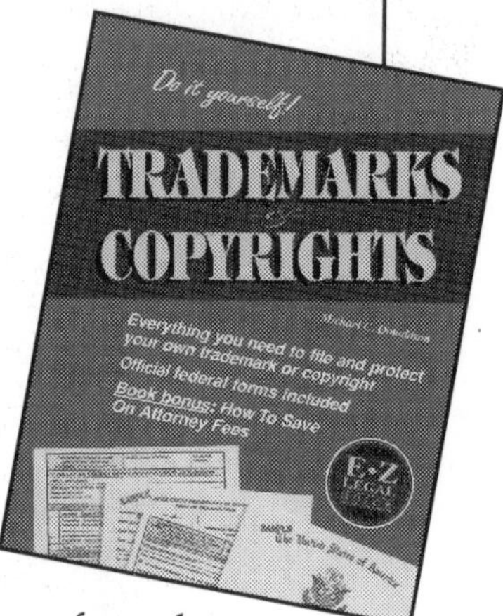

Trademarks and Copyrights

When someone has a great idea and wants to protect it, this book provides the basics of copyright and trademark law: when to get a lawyer, when simply to fill out the right paperwork. Cuts through the volumes of technical information found elsewhere to provide what the layman must know.

Stock No.: G114
$14.95 8.5" x 11"
192 pages Soft cover
ISBN 1-56382-404-3

E•Z Legal Forms Books

A legal library at your fingertips!

When you need it in writing, you need E•Z Legal Forms' comprehensive, simple-to-use form books. Designed for business and home offices as well as for families, each book offers hundreds of forms that can be personalized, adapted or used right from the book. Perforated pages make photocopying easy, and the forms are valid in every state. Available at office supply and bookstores, or call 1-800-822-4566.

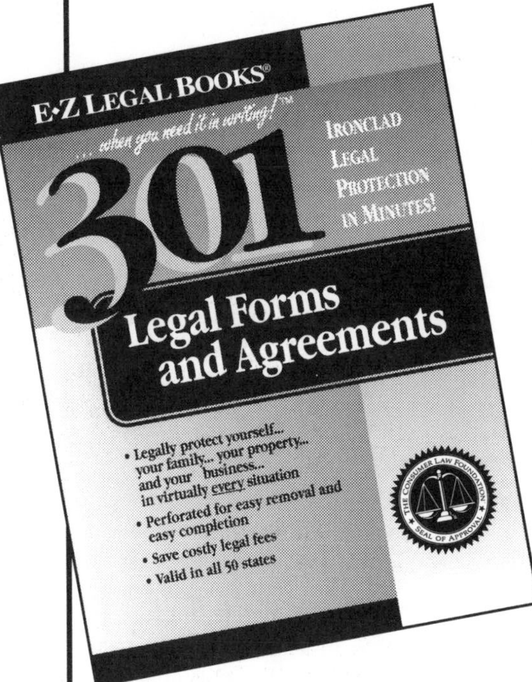

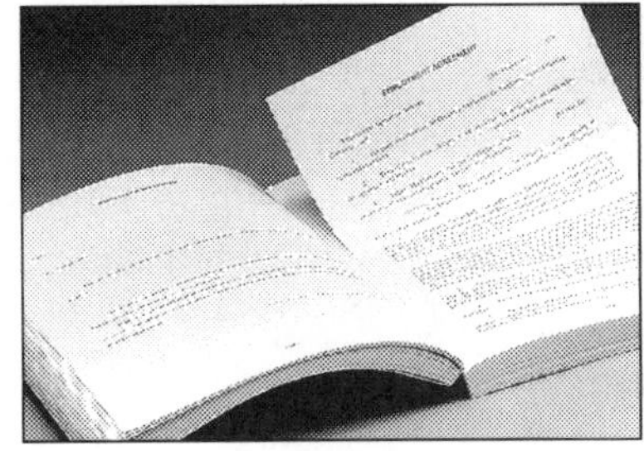

"I have only had 301 Legal Forms and Agreements for a week and it has already saved my business money! Thank you!"
Roger Toups Jr.
Gretna, LA

"301 Legal Forms and Agreements is a wonderful resource. I really like the Promissory Note and the Security Agreement, they're so easy to use."
Ann Yatskowitz
Accion, New Mexico

301 Legal Forms and Agreements

A complete do-it-yourself library of 301 legal documents for virtually every personal or business need, from promissory notes to leases and last wills. Today's consumers know how important it is to protect their families, property, businesses and themselves—and they know they can count on E•Z Legal Forms.

Stock No.: BK301
$24.95 8.5" x 11"
400 pages Soft cover
ISBN 1-56382-301-2

Personnel Director

America's #1 Employee Management System!

Personnel Director manages employees more efficiently, effectively and legally – without expensive legal fees. A collection of over 240 personnel agreements, forms, letters and documents for virtually every size and type of business. Forms document employee turnover, set policy, put agreements in writing and keep all necessary records. Perfect for time-starved small or midsize businesses that want to protect themselves and their employees.

Stock No.: BK302
$24.95 8.5" x 11"
290 pages Soft cover
ISBN 1-56382-302-0

E·Z LEGAL BOOKS®

Corporate Secretary

When business owners are ready to incorporate, they don't need a lawyer, they need *Corporate Secretary*. It provides over 170 minutes, resolutions, notices and other essential documents for companies, whether they are small or midsize, private or public, non-profit or for profit, "S" or "C." Helps any corporation hold regular, official meetings and document the votes and transactions of its directors and shareholders.

Stock No.: BK304
$24.95 8.5" x 11"
270 pages Soft cover
ISBN 1-56382-304-7

Credit Manager

Business owners stop credit losses and get paid with *Credit Manager*, a complete credit and collection system of over 200 letters, agreements, notices, memos and other documents. *Credit Manager* is for any organization that wants to avoid troublesome disputes and legal liability while enforcing its legal rights and fulfilling legal obligations in credit and collections.

Stock No.: BK303
$24.95 8.5" x 11"
260 pages Soft cover
ISBN 1-56382-303-9

Family Record Organizer

Family Record Organizer contains every form the well-organized household needs to keep life running smoothly, from travel planning to family event scheduling to monthly goal setting. Special sections on business records, investment and financial records, and purchase and maintenance records make it perfect for the home business. E-Z Legal's recordkeeping forms organize every aspect of your life.

Stock No.: BK300
$24.95 8.5" x 11"
226 pages Soft cover
ISBN 1-56382-300-4

20 million Americans are in trouble with the IRS

How to settle with the IRS... for pennies on the dollar

Solid advice for worried taxpayers.

Arnold S. Goldstein, Ph.D.

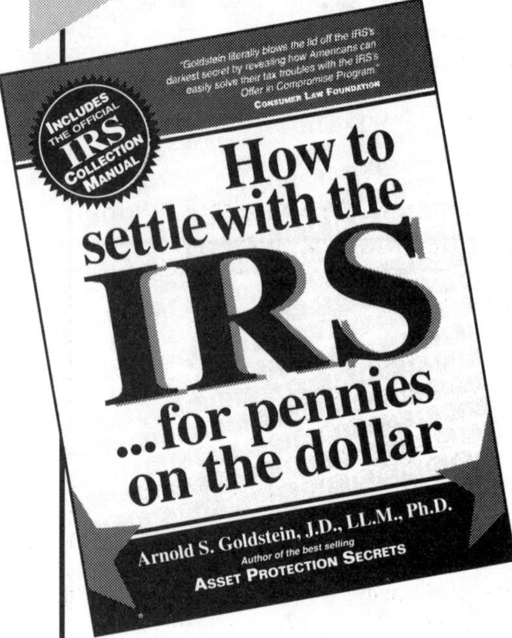

"Goldstein literally blows the lid off the IRS's darkest secret by revealing how Americans can easily solve their tax troubles with the IRS's Offer in Compromise Program."
Consumer Law Foundation

"An invaluable guide to how the IRS really works and how you can reclaim your life when the IRS is after you."
Mark S. Tilden, Attorney, Boston, MA

Stock No.: IRS 200
$19.95 8.5" x 11"
272 pages Soft cover
ISBN 1-880539-13-6

Here's the best selling book that shows taxpayers how to take advantage of the IRS's newly expanded Offer in Compromise Program and save up to 90% or more on their tax bill. Tens of thousands of taxpayers are finding it easier than ever to resolve their tax woes with the tried and true tax saving strategies in this must-have book. The book provides clear and precise answers on how to:

- Protect assets from the IRS.
- Determine if an Offer in Compromise is the best option.
- Plan...even before tax returns are filed.
- Find free and low-cost tax help.
- Settle estate taxes as easily and cheaply as income taxes.
- Look "penniless" to the IRS.
- Gain more time to pay overdue taxes.
- Avoid tax liens.
- Decide when bankruptcy is an option.
- Abate penalties and interest.
- Stop levies and seizures.
- Negotiate your best deal with the IRS.

...and much more!

Available at your nearest bookstore, or call 1-800-822-4566.

GARRETT PUBLISHING, INC.

OUR #1 BEST SELLER

Asset Protection Secrets

This best seller has been featured on over 250 radio and TV shows!

Arnold S. Goldstein, Ph.D.

Asset Protection Secrets reveals all the little-known secrets and perfected strategies guaranteed to protect personal and business assets from financial disaster. This is a full resource guide packed solid with over 230 perfectly legal ways to:

- Become judgment proof.
- Go bankrupt and keep everything!
- Protect assets from IRS seizure.
- Avoid a lawsuit in today's lawsuit-crazy society.
- Leave assets to children so they're fully protected from creditors.
- Shelter property from the IRS, divorce, probate, and creditors.
- Safeguard a business from creditors.
- Shelter wages from attachment.
- Use offshore havens for ironclad financial secrecy and protection.

Dr. Arnold S. Goldstein is among a select group of distinguished experts recognized for his knowledge of tax and financial protection strategies. Featured on over 400 radio and television shows nationwide, he has authored more than 72 books on law, business and finance.

Founder and President of Wealth$avers, an international financial planning and asset protection organization, Dr. Goldstein also conducts Asset Protection Secrets Seminars nationwide. He is Professor Emeritus at Northeastern University, and teaches asset protection strategies at several colleges and universities. He holds the degrees of Bachelor of Science, Master of Business Administration, Doctor of Jurisprudence, Master of Laws and Ph.D. in law and public policy. He is a member of the Massachusetts and federal bars as well as many professional, academic and civic organizations.

"Asset Protection Secrets is a complete encyclopedia of techniques and tactics to safeguard your assets under all circumstances."
Consumer Law Foundation

"The most important personal finance book this century."
Delray Press

"Asset Protection Secrets is awesome. It really shows people how to build a financial fortress around their wealth."
Robert Itzkow
Taxpayer's Assistance Corp.

Newly revised edition... Updated tax laws and more.

Stock No.: GAPS 100
$29.95 8.5" x 11"
360 pages Soft cover
ISBN 1-880539-004

GARRETT PUBLISHING, INC.

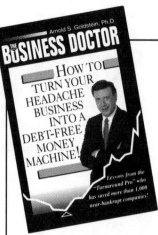

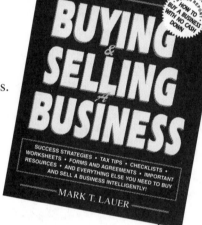

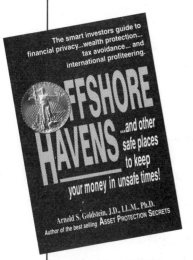

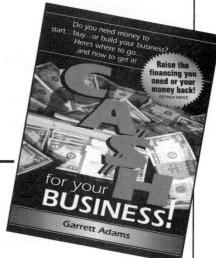

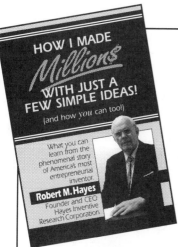

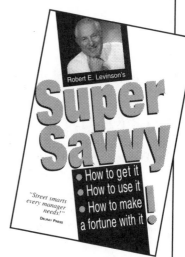

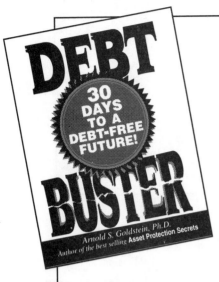

Index

A-C

Account information..........................9, 62, 63
Agent banks..25-26
Annual membership fees........................26-27
Annual percentage rate (APR).....................27
ATM cards...27-28
ATM machines..27
Bank borrowing......................................19-20
Bank card system.......................................24
Bankruptcy, repossession and foreclosure60-61
CBI/Equifax...37
Chain...25
Charge off...35
Checking account..19
Collateral...15, 19, 32
Collection agency.......................................57
Consumer protection...................................27
Consumer Statement...................................36
Credit bureau liability.................................49
Credit cards...23-34
Credit clinics..61-62
Credit denial..36
Credit history....................................11, 20, 22
Credit rating..11-12
Credit report disclosures.........................35-36
Credit report requests..................................35
Credit scoring system..................................12
Creditor cooperation...............................51-56
CSC Credit Services, Inc.............................37

D-W

Debit cards..28
Debit card liability.......................................28
Ding..40
Duplicate account.......................................25
Fair Credit Reporting Act (FCRA)...............39
Federal Trade Commission..........................39
Finance charge..49
Free credit report...49
Grace period..31
Historical status...40
Identification information............................35
Inquiries................................25, 30, 31, 40
Loan officer...11-12
LIBOR..27
Major bank...25-26
Master Credit Data.......................................22
Open account status......................................58
Public record information.............................35
PIN...27
Reasonable time.......................................39, 46
Repayment history..11
Secured credit card...................................18-19
Short-term-debt-to-income ratio....................12
Subscribers..9
Tax liens...59-60
Trans Union Corporation...............................37
Transaction fees...26
TRW Credit Information Service...................37
Twenty percent rule..17
Win-win offer..57-58

NOTES

NOTES

NOTES

NOTES

NOTES